# FEMALE DEITIES IN BUDDHISM

Also by Vessantara
*Meeting the Buddhas*
*Tales of Freedom*
*The Mandala of the Five Buddhas*
*The Vajra and Bell*

Vessantara

# FEMALE DEITIES IN BUDDHISM

## A CONCISE GUIDE

$\textit{w}$

Windhorse Publications
38 Newmarket Road
Cambridge
CB5 8DT
info@windhorsepublications.com
windhorsepublications.com

Cover image based on a photograph of White Tara by Bodhiketu,
   © Clear Vision Trust Picture Archive
Cover design by Vincent Stokes
Printed by Bell & Bain Ltd, Glasgow

British Library Cataloguing in Publication Data:
A catalogue record for this book is available from the British Library

ISBN 9781-899579-53-2

PUBLISHER'S NOTE: Since this work is intended for a general readership, Pali and
Sankrit words have been transliterated without the diacritical marks that would have
been appropriate in a work of a more scholarly nature, except in quotations
and technical contexts.

# CONTENTS

# ILLUSTRATION CREDITS

## Colour plates

## Line drawings

*About the Author*

Vessantara is a senior member of the Western Buddhist Order. Born Tony McMahon in London in 1950, he gained an MA in English at Cambridge University. Interested in Buddhism since his teens, he first had direct contact with Buddhists in 1971. In 1974 he became a member of the Western Buddhist Order and was given the name Vessantara, which means 'universe within'. In 1975 he gave up a career in social work to become chairman of the Brighton Buddhist Centre. Since then he has divided his time between meditating, studying, and aiding the development of several Buddhist centres, including retreat centres in England, Wales, and Spain.

For six years he was secretary to Sangharakshita, the founder of the Western Buddhist Order, and for seven years he led three-month courses for people entering the Order.

He is much in demand as a Buddhist teacher, giving talks and leading retreats and workshops in Europe and Australasia.

# PREFACE

When Windhorse Publications suggested I write a book on female Buddhist deities, I found the idea very interesting indeed. Although there have been studies of particular figures such as Tara or the dakini, I am not aware of any book that brings together the main female figures visualized in the Buddhist tradition. It has been a fascinating process to bring them together here and survey the results. Exploring these varied figures can tell us a great deal: about how Buddhism has related to the feminine, about how deeper aspects of reality can present themselves in female forms, and, above all, about the potential of our own minds as twenty-first-century women and men.

Portia Howe originally came up with the idea of a book that focused on female figures. As a starting point, Jnanasiddhi, my editor at Windhorse, selected extracts from my earlier book, *Meeting the Buddhas: a Guide to Buddhas, Bodhisattvas, and Tantric Deities*. To those extracts I then added a great deal of new material on some fascinating figures for whom there was no room in *Meeting the Buddhas*.

The book has gained greatly from Jnanasiddhi's perceptive, helpful, and encouraging comments as the project unfolded.

Vijayamala read the final draft and suggested several improvements. I'm grateful to Padmavajri, Shantavira, and all the Windhorse team, who work beyond the call of duty to produce Buddhist books to high standards. As an author, I always feel in very safe hands with them.

Although neither of them has been involved in this project, there are two people whom I have to thank for my understanding of Buddhist visualization, and my feeling for these female figures. Sangharakshita has helped me come to know and love these figures over the last thirty years. Dagyab Kyabgon Rinpoche has also been a great help to me in understanding the nature of these figures, and a source of inspiration to meditate on them.

To all the above, and to the many other friends who have contributed to this book, directly or indirectly, I offer my heartfelt thanks.

*Vessantara,*
*Birmingham*
*October 2002*

# 1

## UNEARTHING THE RICHES OF THE MIND

### The Relevance of these Figures for Us

This book deals with figures that are not part of our culture, but that come from India, Tibet, and China. They are also not part of our time, as most of them are at least a thousand years old. Not only that: most of them are not even historical figures from whose lives we can learn, but figures that appeared in the meditations of men and women in the East long ago. So how are they relevant to us? And why are so many thousands of Westerners finding that contact with them has a transforming effect on their lives?

The answers to these questions have to do with the nature of our minds as men and women. We all have our everyday lives and everyday mental states as we go to work, watch television, shop, cook, and so on. But the 'everyday us' is just the tip of the iceberg of consciousness. Modern Western psychology, particularly that of Carl Jung and his followers, has demonstrated what most religions and cultures down the ages have taken for granted: that there are depths to consciousness of which we are mostly unaware. These unconscious depths contain a treasure trove of powerful and meaningful symbols, which Jung called archetypes.

Much of our suffering and feeling of lack of fulfilment in life come from our being out of touch with these deeper, archetypal forces in our minds. If we have no contact with them we can feel that life is empty and meaningless. Or we may contact them indirectly, through psychologically projecting something of their power onto a particular person in the outer world. We can catch ourselves doing this sometimes when we find that we are over-reacting either positively or negatively to another human being. Suddenly we may fall in love with someone, feeling that they have all the qualities we have been looking for in life. Later, when the projection falls away, we feel confused: how could that person who seemed so wonderful and beautiful suddenly have feet of clay and be so ordinary? Or we may project the dark side of the unconscious, so that people at work, or some group, seem powerful tyrants or dangerous enemies, when all the time they are ordinary human beings, perhaps a bit difficult, whom we are investing with our own inner power.

We need to take an interest in our experience to become aware of occasions when it feels as if we are investing the everyday with the archetypal. For instance, I watched the women's tennis final at Wimbledon on TV this year. Watching Serena and Venus Williams battling on court, I realized after a while that they had become overshadowed by various archetypes in my mind. They were no longer two young women hitting balls of inflated rubber with graphite rackets. They were not even two awesome athletes. For me, they had become women warriors battling for victory. This touched on some kind of primeval image in my mind, as if they were just the latest in a whole line of warrior women stretching back through time, and in a sense outside time. For me, the Williams sisters were related to the Amazons – the powerful female warriors of Greek mythology. As they were sisters, another powerful archetypal theme arose, about the struggle of the younger sibling to break free from the elder, to gain her freedom. My mind was adding all this, and more, to the TV pictures of these two women hitting tennis balls around.

In the modern world, we often have no means of making direct, positive contact with these archetypal forces. For many people in the West, traditional religion has become too loaded with unhelpful associations, such as authoritarianism or feelings of guilt. So people are increasingly turning to other sources to help them to contact the deep powers within their own minds. One very rich source of methods for doing this is the Buddhist tradition. Buddhism combines very clear, rational teaching about the nature of life and the mind with powerful methods of meditation and ritual to transform the depths of consciousness. One of its most potent methods is the visualization of archetypal figures, such as the ones we shall be meeting in this book.

You may wonder how you will make an emotional connection with figures that have developed in a completely different culture to ours. But from watching hundreds of Westerners getting to know them over the last thirty years, I can say from my own experience that this is usually no problem at all. These figures are not really Eastern; they are universal. They come from a level of human experience that transcends issues of East and West. Many of the figures we shall meet in this book were first meditated on in India, and subsequently went to Tibet, which was a radically different kind of culture. The Tibetans have happily assimilated these Indian figures, and I am sure that Westerners need have no trouble. Sometimes you may see pictures of these figures with Eastern features that don't appeal to you, but as you dwell on them you find that they subtly change over time, often taking on a rather more Western appearance in your mind. In my experience, the only people who have serious difficulty relating to these figures are those who become caught up with external appearances and tell themselves that the figures come from a different culture. They are wrong. The figures do not come from thousands of miles away. They come from deep levels of your own mind. They are closer to you than your own front door.

Whether we find it easy or difficult to relate to these figures, in a way we have no choice if we are interested in the Buddhist path. Buddhism is such a new arrival in the West that, as yet, we have almost no Western images of what Enlightenment might look like. So we are still at the stage of taking on these traditional images and making them our own. Over time, the Buddhist tradition in the West will develop, and new archetypal figures that communicate what Enlightenment is like will appear, so one day we shall not need to make any cultural leap. But for now, if we want to gain a feeling for the wisdom and compassion, freedom and serenity that Buddhism is aiming at, our best way forward is to spend time with these wonderful female figures that have helped millions of people to contact the rich potential of their own minds.

## How to Use This Book

Some people may just use this book for information, to learn about the different female Buddhist figures, which is fine. You could read the whole thing fairly quickly, and then come back and concentrate on the figures that particularly spoke to you. Or you may find that it works better for you to dip into the book slowly, only reading about one or two figures at a time. In this way, you will give yourself the chance to make a real contact with the figures. In dealing with archetypes, depth is much more important than quantity.

Just knowing about these figures, however, will not have much of a transformative effect on your mind. For any real change to happen, you will need to engage with them imaginatively. You can do this in a formal way by receiving the permission or initiation of one of these figures from a qualified Buddhist teacher and then practising a visualization *sadhana*: a set sequence of visualizations, usually with accompanying verses and mantras. But many people may not have the opportunity, or may not wish to do this for one reason or another. If you have not been formally introduced to any of these figures, there is nothing wrong in getting some sense of them by using your imagination. So while reading, do try to conjure up the figures in your mind's eye. Try to gain a feeling for them, for their beauty and power, and for the richness of their qualities, such as love and compassion, peace, and wisdom. Just doing that is very helpful and healing for the mind.

As well as trying to imagine the figures while reading, there are many things you can do to strengthen your connection with them, to make them real for you. If you find you are particularly drawn to one of the figures, you can look for pictures of her, or draw or paint her yourself. If I give her mantra – her sound symbol – or you know it, you can either silently recite it to yourself, or chant it aloud. If it feels right for you, you can make a shrine somewhere at home with a picture, some flowers, maybe some incense. You can wear clothes of the colour associated with the figure in her honour. In these ways you will be inviting that figure into your life, expressing your openness to the Enlightened qualities that she embodies.

If you do these things, you will engage with these figures not just with your head but with your heart. You will begin to set in motion new currents in the depths of your being. You may find feelings of love or devotion for some of the figures arising. Follow your intuition. All these figures are embodiments of

Enlightened consciousness. Even those that appear outwardly dangerous are all totally benign and committed to helping all living beings. Contemplating and reflecting on them will enrich your life.

I have tried to make life as easy as possible for readers who do not know much about Buddhism. However, there are a few new words to learn, as some traditional Buddhist terms do not easily translate into English. Also, in the original languages the names of some of the figures are a bit long and daunting. I have tried to ease into things gradually, but the Sanskrit or Tibetan names are in frequent use in Buddhist circles in the West, so I could not just use English translations all the time. I have tried to cater for different kinds of readers by putting some of the information that is not relevant to newcomers in the notes at the end of the book. I have also tried to write in a way that is accessible to both women and men. The Buddha believed that all human beings have the potential to gain Enlightenment. Whatever your gender, race, nationality, or background, these Buddhist figures are relevant to your mind, and this book is for you.

### *Female* Figures

Though I have said that these figures are relevant to everyone, women may nonetheless be particularly glad to have such a range of powerful female archetypes brought together in one place. Although these figures are female symbols, and that is not the same thing as gender, women may naturally feel particularly at ease and connected with some of these female figures, compared to their male counterparts. Western women often grow up feeling rather impoverished in the area of positive female role models. In these pages you will come upon the most positive models imaginable. All these female figures embody the qualities of Enlightenment, but they do so in many different forms, from the young and beautiful to the old and the dangerous. There are female figures here that mirror many different aspects of women's experience of life, but they are all clear, shining mirrors, all expressions of the Enlightened mind.

For men, these figures will tend to represent Enlightenment filtered through the forms of the anima, the feminine aspect of the male psyche. Jungian psychology has shown that both men and women have the potential to develop the whole range of masculine and feminine psychological qualities. However, the qualities associated with the opposite sex are usually deeply unconscious. This complementary female element in a man is what Jung termed the anima. (The equivalent masculine element in a woman is the animus.) The anima may appear in dreams or imagination, but it is often projected onto women in the outside world – which can cause a great deal of confusion. A man may find himself drawn at times to different figures, depending upon which aspect of the anima has the most pulling power for him. It could be the queen, the warrior woman, the lover, or the shamaness/magician.

Thus all these figures can teach us something about who we are as men and women. But although it can be very helpful to think in terms of archetypes, the anima, and other psychological terms, we must be very careful not to reduce these figures to pawns, or even queens, to be moved around on our psychological chessboard. We are dealing here with living forces. In fact we are dealing with our deepest and most sacred potential as human beings – our capacity to develop beyond all suffering and to become ourselves embodiments of love, compassion, wisdom, and freedom.

## Relating to the Figures

Before we start to engage with these female Buddhist figures, it is important that we try to gain a sense of what they are. I refer to them as 'deities' and sometimes as 'goddesses', but what do these words mean here? Are these figures externally existent – out there in the universe somewhere – or just aspects of our own minds? Neither of these two ways of looking at the question really does justice to the truth of the matter. Perhaps the best way to put it is that these figures represent potentials of our own minds, but not of our own egos.

In Buddhist texts there are several teaching stories of people who believe they are poor when actually they are very rich. In one story someone has a friend who sews a precious jewel into their clothing for them, but for long years they never find it. In another there is a child who has wandered away from home and lives by begging, while in the meantime their parent has become fabulously wealthy and longs to share their riches with their child. Both the stories end happily, with the poor person discovering their wealth, but only after long years of separation.

These stories provide a good description of our situation. We all have the riches of Enlightenment as a potential within our minds, but because we usually stay on the surface levels of our experience, we feel impoverished, wandering from one situation to another, trying to find satisfaction. We do not remember or recognize our connection to our inner riches. As the Zen master Hakuin's *Song of Meditation* goes:

> *Not knowing it is near, they seek it afar. What a pity!*
> *It is like one in the water who cries out for thirst;*
> *It is like the child of a rich house who has strayed away among the poor.*[1]

These deep and rich levels of the mind are always there and, in a sense, are always aware of us and never forget us. The archetypal figures we shall be meeting are like messengers from those deep inner levels, coming to give us a sense of the vast riches within. But inevitably, when we enter into relationship with these figures, we feel at first as though they have nothing to do with us. As long as we are living on the surface of life, limited mainly to egotistical concerns, we can only interpret these figures as external deities, but the more that we interact with them, the more we shall realize that we are intimately connected with them. By relating to these figures we are led into an exploration of the depths of consciousness. As a result, we shall eventually discover all the riches hidden in our minds. We shall become totally identified with the love, compassion, peace, and freedom that these figures embody.

Thus we can say that these female deities are 'in here' in the sense that over time we can become one with them; we can become embodiments of Enlightened qualities ourselves. But as we have not yet owned the qualities that they embody they will start by feeling external to us. They will feel separate from us, and seem to have qualities that we do not possess. So we should not understand words like 'female deity' or 'goddess' too literally; these figures do not exist in some heavenly realm. At the same time, when we talk about them as aspects of our minds we should not treat them as merely symbolic, or as 'figments of our imagination' in the way that most people in the West use those terms. These figures can have as much impact on us as a 'real person'.

If you find all this rather hard to grasp, it is best simply not to worry about it. Relate to the figures in whatever way feels most natural to you. The main thing is that you make a relationship with them. If you do that, then over time the nature of the figures will become clear to you. However you think about them, if you engage with these figures you will find that they have an impact on your life, on who you are. If you interact with them on a regular basis, you will discover they have a profoundly positive effect. One of the axioms of Buddhism is that you tend to become what you turn your mind towards. So if you keep bearing in mind these female embodiments of wisdom and compassion they will come to play an increasingly valuable part in your life. As a result, your responses to people and situations will become wiser and more loving.

## Where Do These Female Deities Come From?

Paradoxically, the trail that leads to these female figures starts with a man. Gautama the Buddha lived in northern India approximately 2,500 years ago. He was born into a rich family, but as he grew up he became increasingly concerned with questions about life, and especially with how to avoid its sufferings and frustrations. Eventually he decided to leave home and search for freedom, for answers to the existential questions that would not leave him alone. After living as a homeless wanderer for six years, and trying various methods of meditation as well as extreme ascetic practices, he finally gained Enlightenment in deep meditation on the bank of the Nairanjana River. This experience answered all his questions. He had attained a state of complete understanding of the nature of things. Along with that understanding came an overwhelming love and compassion for all living things, as well as the knowledge that he was permanently free from any form of mental suffering. After he had spent some time absorbing that overwhelming experience the Buddha began to teach. He spent the remaining forty-five years of his life travelling around northern India helping others to become Enlightened.

After the Buddha died at the age of 80, his followers naturally remembered him. They often imagined him as he had been in life – endlessly kind and understanding, and fiercely energetic in helping others to understand the true nature of things, to gain 'insight into reality' as it was sometimes called. They pictured him gaining Enlightenment, seated cross-legged in deep meditation.

Over time something very interesting began to happen. People who became very concentrated while imagining the figure of the Buddha found that their mental images came increasingly to life. They became more like visions of the Buddha. These visions were so compelling that they had a profoundly positive effect on their minds. It was as if they had actually met the Buddha. Afterwards they would sometimes share these experiences with others, describing how the Buddha looked in their vision. Their descriptions then came to form the basis on which other people meditated on the Buddha. By calling the Buddha to mind in the form that had been described, they would try to achieve their own powerful mental meetings with him. So in this way a whole tradition of visualizing the Buddha grew up.

As the centuries passed, further developments came about. Some people found that the Buddha was giving them teachings in their meditations, and wrote these down so that new Buddhist texts appeared. Not only that, the forms the Buddha took on in these visionary meditations sometimes altered. He would appear in different positions, holding various emblems, or even with his body radiating light of various colours. All these features, seen in profound states of concentration, took on tremendous symbolic meaning for those who saw them.

Eventually, some of these meditative forms became so very different from the original that they were conceived of as other Buddhas. The idea came about that there were a multiplicity of forms of Enlightened being, and that it was possible to contact them through inner concentration. Buddhist meditators, engaged in profound pioneering in unexplored reaches of the mind, found that they contained whole universes with endless numbers of Buddha forms. Not only Buddhas: there were other spiritual beings who might not be fully Enlightened but who were far advanced on the Buddhist path and who were devoting themselves out of compassion to the welfare of living beings. These great figures were known as Bodhisattvas: 'Beings of Enlightenment'.

As the historical Buddha had been born male, the natural tendency was to visualize Buddhas and Bodhisattvas in male form. However, the state of Enlightenment transcends biological distinctions. It happens on a plane of consciousness on which physical gender is completely irrelevant. So sometimes the visions of these supposedly male figures were so subtle, so refined, that they appeared androgynous, having all positive qualities, masculine and feminine.

Eventually the situation became very fluid indeed. Occasionally a Bodhisattva who had originally been visualized in male form transformed into a female figure. Even more important, female figures of Buddhas and Bodhisattvas started to appear that were understood to be as valid manifestations of the Enlightened mind as their male counterparts.

The rich mix of these meditations was enhanced by further elements. Over the centuries, other great teachers of Buddhism were sometimes visualized in the same way that the historical Buddha had been. Some of these great teachers were female. In addition, as Buddhism spread throughout India and beyond, it encountered many other spiritual traditions, many of whom worshipped their own local gods and goddesses. When people of these traditions became converted to Buddhism, the deities they had worshipped sometimes became incorporated into Buddhist meditations. This could happen because Buddhism is a non-theistic religion. The Buddha was not a god or some kind of incarnation of God, he was a human being who had found the path to total freedom. The wisdom and compassion whose sources he discovered could be expressed through many different symbolic figures. In this way, some indigenous goddesses came to be regarded as forms of Buddhas or Bodhisattvas, and were added to the riches of the Buddhist treasury of meditation practices.

The form of Buddhism in which these female figures started to appear was known as the Mahayana – the 'Great Way'. In the centuries after the Buddha's death, some of his followers came to identify serious practice of Buddhism almost exclusively with monasticism. The Mahayana regarded this as too narrow, and stressed that all those who made sincere efforts could make great progress on the path to Enlightenment. Mahayana Buddhism flowered in India until the twelfth century, when it was wiped out by the Muslim invaders. Thankfully it was transmitted to large parts of Asia, including Tibet and China. Nearly all the figures we shall be meeting in the coming chapters have been visualized by Tibetan Buddhists until the present day. The one exception is Kuan Yin, who is a figure that originated in China.

From around the seventh century, many Indian practitioners of Mahayana Buddhism began using Tantric methods to increase the effectiveness of their Buddhist practice. (The Tantras had appeared much earlier, but it took some time for them to be used as a means for gaining Enlightenment, rather than for mundane magic.) Buddhist Tantra is a methodology for transforming consciousness in its depths. It employs many forms of non-rational and symbolic practices to bring the message of Enlightenment to levels of the mind that are left largely untouched by even the clearest rational teachings. Tantra uses symbolic ritual, mantras, *mudras* (symbolic gestures), the visualization of mandalas (sacred spaces), and many other methods. It also employs a great deal of sexual imagery, using visualizations of deities locked in sexual embrace to symbolize blissful states of Enlightened consciousness.

The Tantra gave greater freedom and higher value to women than some other forms of Buddhism. It was also extremely fruitful in producing new forms of meditation on symbolic figures. Thus many of the figures we shall be meeting here either originated from, or were incorporated into, Buddhist Tantric meditation. As the Buddhist Tantra developed it gave increasing importance to the feminine. Indeed, the final major development of Buddhist Tantra in India was the appearance of Yogini Tantras. (A yogini is a female practitioner of yoga.) These began to appear during the ninth and tenth centuries, and derive their name from the important and distinctive place they accord to female figures.

So the figures we shall be encountering in the coming chapters have been around for a very long time. Their meditations have been tried and tested by many generations of Buddhists. And now they have come to the West, to help more men and women to discover the riches of their minds. Let us start to meet them.

# 2

## THE MANY FORMS OF TARA

## Green Tara: Quintessence of Compassion

We shall begin with one of the best known and best loved female figures in the whole of Buddhism. The Bodhisattva Tara is compassion at its most gentle and heartfelt. She is the most popular female deity in Tibetan Buddhism. There are many thousands of meditational deities in Tibetan Buddhism, many of whom would only be known to lamas who specialize in their meditations. But every Tibetan can recognize the smiling and beautiful form of Tara, and her mantra is very frequently on their lips.

Devotion to her permeates Tibetan society. She is invoked by people wanting help in domestic difficulties, and by those making long and dangerous Himalayan journeys. In the Tibetan summer, before the Chinese takeover of the country, there would often be events lasting several days which were a mixture of a picnic party and a religious festival. As well as the feasting and story-telling, monks would perform offering rituals to Tara, and everybody would join in the chanting of verses of homage to her, which almost everyone knew by heart. At the more esoteric end of the scale, in her form known as Cittamani – 'jewel of the mind' – Tara is often meditated on in the complex yogas of Highest Tantra, which can lead to full Enlightenment in a single lifetime.

Tara has taken on many forms over the centuries, and we shall explore several of them in this chapter. We shall begin by looking at the most common form of all: Green Tara. It may seem strange to imagine a goddess whose body is made of green light, but we are concerned here not with naturalism, but with inner spiritual experience. On deep levels of the mind, figures can appear in different colours, each with their own symbolic meaning. In this chapter we shall meet forms of Tara of several different colours. When you imagine it in your mind's eye, each colour conveys a different kind of emotional tone, a different spiritual message. Green is a calming and soothing colour, which suggests that the green form of Tara is particularly effective for those who want to overcome anxiety and develop fearlessness.

## Tara's Birth and Her Vow to Remain in Female Form

As well as appearing in meditation practices, many of the female figures we shall meet in this book have over the centuries acquired a whole lore about them, such as stories of how they first appeared, or ways in which they have helped people who were devoted to them. This is particularly true of Tara. In this section we shall look at the stories of how she was born, and also at how she came to be a Bodhisattva in female form.

To see Tara's first manifestation in the world, we need to imagine the Bodhisattva Avalokita appearing in the cloudless blue sky.[2] He is a male figure who particularly embodies compassion. His body is pure white, shining against the blueness. From his vantage point in the sky he looks out over the world. For endless thousands of years his principal meditation has been to reflect on the sufferings of living beings, and his only concern has been helping them to overcome that suffering. Seeing that despite all his efforts there is still so much pain and heartache everywhere, he begins to shed tears. The tears fall to earth and form a great lake. From the lake grows a pale blue lotus flower, and on the lotus appears a princess, her body made of green light.

The jade eyelids of the princess open for the first time to reveal two perfect blue eyes, identical to those from which she was born. She looks out over the world and the lake of tears wept by Avalokita, and upward to the white cloud of compassion far above her, and her face breaks into a smile of such beauty and tenderness that the whole world trembles with joy.

From her heart rays of light begin to pour forth. Shining through the rain of compassionate tears still falling around her they produce myriad rainbows, arcing and dancing in all directions. Every rainbow whispers a sound. They carry it like messengers out from her heart. They whisper the sound to the troubled waters of the lake, which become soothed and still. They whisper it to the falling teardrops, which reverse their direction and turn into precious offerings to the cloud of compassion high above them. The rainbows whisper the sound to the universe, to you and me. The sound is the mantra *om tare tuttare ture svaha*. It is the mantra of the beautiful green princess. It is the beginning of the end of all our suffering.

Tara is jade green in colour, clad in a rainbow skirt, with a meditation sash tied around her body. She is decked in precious jewels: bracelets, armlets, anklets, necklaces, earrings, and a tiara of gems. She is seated on a moon mat, her left foot resting on her right thigh in meditation posture. Her right foot steps down gracefully, and as it does so a small pastel blue lotus and a moon mat rise out of the lake to form a footrest. Her right arm reaches down, the back of her hand resting on her right knee. Her palm is open in a gesture of supreme giving. Her left hand is held in front of her heart, palm outwards, the thumb and ring finger to-gether, so that the other three fingers point upwards. This ges-ture bestows protection and fearlessness through invoking the Three Jewels – the three great treasures of Buddhism: the Buddha, his teaching, and his Enlightened followers. Tara's thumb and ring finger delicately hold the stem of a lotus flower, which curves upwards to open into a spray of blossoms by her left shoulder. There is a bud, a half-opened flower, and a fully-opened blossom of pale blue. She is sixteen years old, full-breasted, with flowing black hair and perfect blue eyes. She is supremely beautiful.

Her birth from Avalokita's tears is one version of how Tara came into existence. Another legend gives a different account of how Tara came to be a Bodhisattva in female form. An immeasur-able period of time ago, in a world-system called Manifold Light, lived a princess whose name was Moon of Knowledge. She was devoted to the Buddha of that world, who was called Lord of the Drum[3]. She made vast offerings to that Buddha and his retinue, and finally developed the great wish to gain Enlightenment for the sake of all living beings.[4]

Some monks then urged her to pray to be reborn in a male body to follow her career as a Bodhisattva. The early Buddhists generally believed that it was easier to follow the Buddhist path as a man. So although the Buddha had some great and Enlightened female followers, it was common for women to be seen as disadvantaged in the spiritual life. This view partly re-flected the values of Indian society at the time. It also took into account that many serious Buddhist practitioners lived outside conventional society as homeless wanderers. Obviously it would be more dangerous for a woman to meditate or walk the forest paths alone. However, the princess would have none of the monks' arguments. Her understanding went so deep that she saw that male and female were both concepts projected onto experience, having no existence in ultimate reality. She doubtless also saw the discouraging effect that these views sometimes had on women. So she made a great vow, saying, 'There are many who desire Enlightenment in a man's body, but none who work for the benefit of sentient beings in the body of a woman. Therefore, until mundane existence is empty, I shall work for the benefit of sentient beings in a woman's body.'

Moon of Knowledge then stayed in her palace practising meditation, until she reached a state of deep meditation called 'saving all sentient beings'. By entering into this unimaginably powerful state of concentration, she rescued every morning and evening a million million sentient beings from mundane existence. As a result she became known as Tara, the Saviouress.

## The Qualities of Tara

Tara can mean 'star' – but it is usually understood to mean 'saviouress' or 'one who ferries across'. This image of ferrying is very common in Buddhism. The Buddha described his teaching as like a raft for crossing a river. On one side, the side on which we currently stand, is the unsatisfactory and unfulfilling world of mundane existence (known as *samsara* in Buddhist tradition). On the other, the 'farther shore', is the complete peace, freedom, and permanent fulfilment of Enlightenment (*nirvana*). Through meditating on Tara, who is the embodiment of the Buddha's teaching, you find yourself imperceptibly moving from one shore to the other, being ferried across to safety.

As well as fearlessness, the green form of Tara is especially associated with spontaneous helpfulness. Like a mother instantly and unthinkingly leaping into danger if her child is threatened, Green Tara steps down at once to give aid and protection to any living being who calls on her. This function as protectress extends, in popular Buddhist tradition, far beyond the spiritual realm. Many Tara devotees would call on her or recite her mantra to guard against mundane perils and difficulties as well. For example, Tara is said to protect one from the eight great terrors: lions, elephants, fire, snakes, robbers, captivity, shipwreck, and demons. Sometimes this list is understood symbolically, as relating to the spiritual dangers of pride, delusion, anger, envy, wrong views, avarice, attachment, and doubt, respectively. However, many people take the idea quite literally, and there is a wealth of Indian and Tibetan stories to attest to the magical way in which, through calling on Tara, people have escaped extreme physical danger. Because of her protective powers Tara was especially popular with merchants and traders, who often ran great risks on their journeys. Perhaps some of the rapid spread of devotion to Tara can be explained by the fact that such people, who had learned to call upon her in times of danger, became in effect her travelling emissaries.

Traditionally, Tara is compared to a virgin, a mother, and a queen. She is like a virgin inasmuch as she is completely pure. She is unstained by the mundane. Her morality is unblemished. On a metaphysical level, too, she is pure. Her wisdom is as eternally fresh as the pastel sky-lotus on which she sits. Arising out of emptiness, she is pure of any conception of inherent existence. Virginity and chastity are also symbols of wholeness and independence. Tara is spiritually complete in herself. The experience of her wisdom and compassion needs no addition or complement.

As we have seen, she has a mother's compassion and an instant response to suffering. She cares for all beings as though each were her only child. Like a mother she is very accepting. So it is said that if you are very tired one morning and get up too late to perform more than an abbreviated version of her meditation, Tara does not mind. She is always understanding and forgiving. (Perhaps even if you write about her, and fail to do her beauty justice, she will understand. Hopefully she will find a way to communicate something of herself anyhow.)

Finally, Tara is like a queen. She exercises spiritual sovereignty. She is dignified and fearless. She takes responsibility for the whole universe, and lays down the law of the Dharma, to bring an end to suffering everywhere.

## Tara in Buddhist Tradition

Tara's history can be traced in such books as Stephan Beyer's *The Cult of Tārā*. (One of the advantages of being a Tara devotee is that there is probably more to read about her in Western languages than about any other Buddha or Bodhisattva figure.) The attention paid to Tara by Western scholars reflects the tremendous devotion shown her by Tibetans. In Indian Buddhism too she gathered enough of a following to appear in many different forms. Green Tara is the most commonly represented and meditated upon, though there are many meditations of White Tara, associated with long life, whom we shall meet later in this chapter.

In Tibetan history, one name stands out above all others in connection with Tara, and that is Atisha. Atisha is a central figure in Tibetan Buddhism. He was invited to Tibet in the eleventh century, when Buddhism there was in decline. When he received the invitation, Atisha was a famous teacher at one of the largest monastic universities in India. Ever since his childhood he had had visions of Tara, and he always felt himself under her care and guidance. So when he was asked to go to Tibet, which from an Indian point of view was not an attractive offer – a country in 'the back of beyond' involving an arduous and dangerous journey – he naturally asked the advice of Tara. She told him that if he went to Tibet it would shorten his life, but he would be of great benefit to people there. Having absorbed much of Tara's kindness and compassion over the years, he naturally decided to go. In Tibet his deep love and devotion for Tara communicated itself to everyone he met. It is from the crystal spring of Atisha's practice that so much of the devotion to Tara in Tibet flowed.

## Tara as the Quick Way to Wisdom

A piece of Buddhist lore about Tara states that she offers 'the quick way to wisdom'. Through meditating on her, insight into reality can be easily and swiftly attained. At first sight this seems paradoxical. Tara is, after all, the quintessence of compassion. So why should she, of all the Bodhisattvas, be regarded as the bestower of rapid understanding of the true nature of things? Many people have found meditation on Tara a very quick vehicle for arriving at insight. This becomes easier to understand if we realize that insight is not an achievement of the rational mind. It is the product of a deep focusing of our energies. We have to unite our head and our heart, our thinking and feeling, into one faculty, and use that to pierce through the veil of wrong ideas and confused emotions to a direct encounter with things as they are. So gaining insight has just as much to do with opening the heart as with developing the intellect.

One of Tara's special attributes is the speed with which she acts. A famous song of praise to her begins 'Homage, Tara, quick one, heroine'. She moves rapidly to help you to escape from samsara, and it is wisdom which allows you to do this, so that is what she quickly bestows.

One of the reasons her visualization is so effective is that she is such an intensely beautiful figure. This means that you want to contemplate her. The more you enjoy her beauty, the more time you will want to spend contemplating her. The longer you spend with her the more her message of loving care for all that lives will communicate itself to you. 'What you set your heart upon, that you become,' according to Buddhism. Spellbound by Tara, lost in her loveliness, you become steadily more Tara-like. You come closer to compassion, and with that you move steadily towards wisdom.

The ten-syllable mantra, *om tare tuttare ture svaha*, is common to nearly all the forms of Tara. It has no rational meaning; it is a play on the sound of Tara's name. Nonetheless, its associations are profound. According to one tradition, this mantra – being the sound-essence of Tara the saviouress – expresses all her powers of swift rescuing. With *tare* we are delivered from all worldly sufferings. With *tuttare* we are liberated from conditioned existence itself. With *ture* we are prevented from falling into a one-sided view of Enlightenment. We are rescued from the danger of seeing nirvana as something to attain for ourselves alone. *Ture* opens our heart to embrace the Bodhisattva ideal, of gaining Enlightenment in order to help all sentient beings do the same. (Thus we could say that *ture* ensures that we shall develop compassion, and hence that we shall eventually become Tara, who is the quintessential experience of compassion. To try to gain Enlightenment purely for our own sake means we shall fail to achieve Tara's blissful state.)

## Beyond the Form of Tara

Tara is very approachable. The lotus on which she sits grows out of a pool on the earth. Tara is Enlightenment stepping down to us, reaching out a hand to lift us up. She is emptiness clothed in its finest raiment. However, her accessibility can cause misunderstandings. Because she is Enlightenment presenting itself to us in such a familiar and attractive disguise, we can easily fail

to see her true nature. For men she may function as an anima figure, for women as a role model, and for both sexes as a form of
earth or nature goddess. However, she is not defined by any of
these views, and finally she is none of, and more than, any of
them. She is the embodiment of transcendental compassion. She is
the inconceivable, the unknowable, the ungraspable, presenting
itself to us in a way that is easy for us poor mortals to relate to. This
is made clear by the fact that her whole body is translucent, made
of light, yet appearing empty, neither existent nor non-existent.

As we see more deeply into her nature, we come to understand
that she is not green, does not hold a lotus, does not reach down
with her right leg. Her beautiful form is just the gateway to a
deep inner experience that has neither colour, nor form, nor gender. The external appearance of Tara is just a molehill hiding a
mountain of Enlightened qualities. So Tara is at the same time
easily approachable and fathomless, familiar yet beyond
understanding.

## White Tara: the Seven Eyes of Wisdom

We have met with the green form of Tara, but she also has a white
form that is very important in the Buddhist Tantric tradition.
How can we picture her? She is seated, in the midst of the sky, on
a white moon mat, spread on a white lotus throne. Like her
green sister, she appears as a young girl, sixteen years old, graceful and very beautiful. Her body is made of white light, like sunlight on snow. She is dressed in delightful silks and jewels. Her
legs are crossed in what Buddhist Tantra calls the vajra posture,
but which we tend to know in the West as the full-lotus posture.
Looking out from the upturned sole of each foot is a wisdom eye.
Her right hand rests on her right knee, turned outwards to give
to all beings. In its palm is another eye. Her left hand is held in

front of her breast in the gesture of bestowing protection. With it she holds the stem of a spray of white lotus flowers. This hand too has an eye in its palm. She has long sleek black hair which falls over her shoulders. Her compassionate smile drowns the world in happiness. In her forehead, placed vertically, is a seventh beautiful eye. Her body is empty, she feels as light as thistledown. Above her head, her guru, the red Buddha Amitabha, whose name means 'boundless light', sits in deep meditation, pouring love into the sky around him, as a shining ruby gives light.

White Tara is surrounded by a great circle of white light – a full moon aura. According to one interpretation, this stands for pacification and the increase of inexhaustible bliss. Through being endowed with this aura, White Tara becomes a moon goddess. The moon is not only beautiful, it is peaceful and benign, shining gently on the world, easy to gaze upon. Its being a full moon strengthens White Tara's magical capacity for increasing things, for enabling them to grow to their fullest possible extent. Through devotion to her, the moon of our life, positive qualities and wisdom finally becomes complete, a perfect circle.

The lotus blossoms in her left hand are usually white, though they can also be the pale blue night lotus, known as *utpala*. There are three flowers, in various stages of development: one still a bud, one half open, and one fully open. In general, lotuses are symbols of growth and development – of leaving behind lower states and growing towards what is higher. The Tara devotee aspires to leave the endless cycle of birth and death behind and arrive at the perfect understanding of Enlightenment. However, these three lotuses can also be reminders of the empty, ungraspable nature of things. One traditional method for realizing this is to consider the nature of the three times: past, present, and future. The past, the fully open lotus bloom, has already passed away; the future, the bud, has not yet revealed itself; the present, symbolized by the half open flower, is as ephemeral as a lightning-flash.

White Tara's seven eyes are mysterious. They suggest the need for compassion to be wise, to see clearly and objectively, otherwise it is mere pity or sentimentality. The explanation given in a meditation quoted by Stephan Beyer is that the seven eyes stand for the four *brahma viharas* and the three *vimokshas*.[5] The four *brahma viharas* are positive emotions. The first one, the root of them all, is loving-kindness. When it encounters suffering, this altruistic love is transformed into compassion – empathizing with another's pain or loss. When it encounters happiness, loving-kindness changes into sympathetic joy – rejoicing in others' merits or good fortune. When these positive feelings have been developed equally to all living beings then you have equanimity, the last of the four. The three *vimokshas* (or 'releases') are insights into different aspects of reality.

In my own mind, however, I have come to associate the eyes with awareness. There is a fundamental Buddhist practice known as 'guarding the gates of the senses'. This consists in trying to be aware, all the time if possible, of what you are taking in through the senses and how it affects you. Buddhism counts the senses as six. There are the usual five and the 'everyday mind' that cognizes ideas, memories, and fantasies. So, for me, there are six eyes to stand guard over the senses, including the mind sense, to ensure that what they perceive does not catalyse anything of our unhelpful or unethical tendencies. What about the seventh eye? Well, that must be the highest eye, in the middle of the forehead, which looks beyond the senses altogether, to perceive transcendental reality, the experience of an Enlightened being, directly. So the seven eyes together suggest awareness permeating all levels of your being.

The eyes can be seen almost like breaches in the skin. This suggests that wisdom can break through in unexpected ways. Perhaps the symbolism of the seven eyes points to the fact that White Tara's whole body is wisdom and awareness.

## Cheating Death

According to the Buddhist Tantric tradition, White Tara offers us the gift of longevity.[6] It is considered a useful power in Buddhism for two reasons. The first is simply that if you are trying to follow the Bodhisattva path, time is precious. The longer you live, the more people you can help.

The second reason concerns your motivation for spiritual practice. Generally speaking, there are two motivations that engage the energy of a human being. The first is the desire for survival, which can take more refined forms, such as the desire for success, riches, fame, sex, and security. Chasing after these is what the Buddha called 'the ignoble quest' – being yourself impermanent and liable to suffering, you go in search of what is also impermanent and unsatisfactory. As we all know, despite its limitations the 'ignoble quest' usually engages a great deal of our energy and interest. The other motivation is the desire for growth and development, the search for Enlightenment, which once attained is permanent and totally satisfying. This is what the Buddha called 'the noble quest'.

Spiritual practice consists in moving energy from the ignoble towards the noble quest. This is no easy task. There may even be times when we fall between two stools. After we have been practising Buddhism for a while, we may find that we are no longer so excited by the everyday world, but we are not yet gaining much emotional nourishment from our spiritual path, so we may become a little becalmed and uninspired, and even feel we have less energy than our friends who have aims no higher than succeeding in business or saving up for holidays and new furniture. If we keep practising the Dharma, though, we shall eventually plant our feet more firmly on the spiritual path, and find we are deriving more energy from spiritual life than we ever did from the ignoble quest.

How wonderful it would be, though, if we could avoid this awkward transition. If we could find a method that engaged both our desire for spiritual development and the energy we usually invest in the struggle for survival, our practice would be really powerful and wholehearted. One way in which we can do this is by visualizing the figure of White Tara. As a Bodhisattva, Tara can rally all the parts of ourselves that are excited by the quest for Enlightenment. In addition, the white form of Tara bestows the gift of long life on her devotees. So those aspects of your being that are concerned with survival are also highly motivated to devote themselves to her.

## The Buddhist View of Factors that Influence Your Lifespan

We now need to ask the question: does the practice work? And if so, how does meditating on White Tara increase your lifespan? There is no way of proving that it does, though many Buddhist meditators firmly believe in it. However, modern medicine is finding increasing evidence of psychological factors underlying disease, so it is not unreasonable to suppose that a practice that produces concentrated and positive mental images and volitions will have a healing effect on the body.

Will-power is becoming increasingly recognized in the West as a factor affecting length of life. It has always been a tenet of popular songs and poetry that you can die of a broken heart or because you have nothing left to live for. More recently, a statistical survey showed that far more old people die shortly after their birthdays than in an equivalent period before it – suggesting that their determination to be present at the celebration keeps them going.

From the Buddhist point of view, there are said to be a number of reasons, or underlying conditions, that cause life to come to an end. One of these is that your physical vitality and energy may no longer be sufficient to sustain life. You lose your physical robustness and cannot withstand disease. As we shall see later, one attribute of White Tara's sadhana is that she is very calming and stilling. Meditation has the effect of concentrating energy and conserving and building up a reservoir of physical vitality.

Buddhism believes that there are also more subtle conditions at work. Through the law of karma you create the world you live in. Each of your mental states calls into being an experience that is its objective counterpart. Human life is considered a great opportunity, which has been brought about by the development of states of love, contentment, and understanding in the past.[7] So if, as a human being, you no longer create sufficient positive mental states, or the volitions that caused you to be born as a human being are exhausted, then, according to the tradition, your life as a human being will come to an end. Meditation on White Tara prevents this from happening since, through identifying yourself with White Tara and her vast compassion for every form of life, you will produce a great stock of positive volitions that ensure that you will live long.[8]

## Higher Goals of Meditating on White Tara

By this point some of you may be thinking that White Tara meditation is all very well, but it does not aim high enough. For a

Buddhist, a long life may be very pleasant, but in itself it is of little value. After all, the *Dhammapada*, a fundamental Buddhist text, says, 'Better than a hundred years lived unaware of the Deathless State is one single day lived aware of the Deathless State.'[9]

Although meditation on White Tara may well give long life, developing longevity is not its central aim. Rather, it is a tremendous bonus, which boosts the energy you can put into the meditation by enabling you to channel your lower, survival-oriented energies into it. What the practice is really about is clearly demonstrated by the White Tara mantra: *om tare tuttare ture mama ayuh punya jnana pushtim kuru svaha.*

This is the basic Tara mantra we met with earlier, with an extra phrase inserted into it. There are many phrases that can be included in the basic mantra to make it effective for particular purposes. This is the most common, and is associated particularly with White Tara. It means 'increase my life, merits, and wisdom'. Here we have a key to the practice. Through meditating on White Tara we realize that human life (*ayus*) is valuable because it gives us the chance to develop merits, or positive qualities, (*punya*) and wisdom (*jnana*), and to help others to do the same.

Dwelling upon long life also involves dwelling upon impermanence, dwelling upon death. So the practice subtly accustoms us to our own mortality; it makes us aware that even a long life must come to an end, and that it is vital to use whatever time we have to build our ship of death (as D. H. Lawrence calls it), and load it with the provisions of merits and wisdom.

Finally, if our practice goes deep enough, White Tara bestows not just long life, but eternal life. We come to realize that even long life is not enough. We are really seeking, through performing the practice, to come to a place where there is no death. This search for the deathless state is the 'noble quest', the search for nirvana. After the Buddha had gained Enlightenment and decided to teach, he said, 'Open are the doors of the Deathless.'[10]

This is the real goal of meditating on White Tara: to help ourselves and all others to be liberated from the Wheel of Life (which is the Wheel of Death), and to attain the deathless state." The final and highest gift that White Tara bestows is the attainment of Enlightenment itself.

Now we can see what we might call the central myth of White Tara. Through her practice we gain long life. We buy time. We use that time to help ourselves and others to develop merit and wisdom. Through gaining merit and wisdom we fulfil the requirements for arriving at the deathless state – liberation, nirvana – so that we can then lead others out of samsara to safety.

The process of arriving at the state of Enlightenment through White Tara practice involves a number of different stages. Firstly, through meditation on her we work to concentrate and contain our energies so that they can be progressively refined and sublimated. Gradually, all the crude energy that is usually channelled into survival is led into the practice by the promise of long life, and transmuted into something higher. All the energy that usually flows into sexual attraction and projection is led to fall in love with the bewitching beauty of White Tara, or the compassionate strength of Amitabha, and thus to fall in love with Enlightenment. It too becomes refined.

Step by step the process of alchemical transmutation proceeds. Our human emotions respond to the warmth and love radiated by White Tara and Amitabha, and offer their energies as well to the service of Enlightenment. As our energies become more refined, so the colours and shapes of White Tara become lighter and brighter. The universe reveals itself as a dance of light and colour. As we move deeper into this experience, and come to understand its insubstantial and ungraspable nature, we begin to move into a timeless realm. Eventually we arrive at a point from which we see that both time and space are just functions of consciousness. White Tara represents the unlimited freedom of the mind that is deeply established in this realization. In this experience, death has disappeared.

That timeless experience lies far down the spiritual path. Perhaps paradoxically, I think that for many people the very first insight that White Tara bestows is an appreciation of the importance of time. We need time to develop spiritually. It can take us many years to arrive at a point in our Dharma practice where we are on safe ground, and in no danger of slipping back. We need time to contact what is beyond time. We need time to practise the Bodhisattva path, time to take the Dharma out to a suffering world.

*O loving Tara,*
*Full-moon goddess,*
*Quintessence of compassion,*
*Please take my hand in yours.*
*With your gift-bestowing touch,*
*Cool and soft,*
*Please lead me gently*
*Along the path to the Deathless.*

*Through your loving-kindness*
*May the darkness of my mind*
*Be illumined*
*By a new moon of wisdom.*
*Then, through my never leaving your presence,*
*May that new moon*
*Day by day increase,*
*Shining its light ever more*
*Upon this suffering world.*
*Until, at last,*
*The aura of my life, merits, and wisdom*
*Grown full,*
*My body, speech, and mind*

*Are mixed inseparably with yours*
*In the undying beauty of Enlightenment.*

## White Tara and Green Tara

White Tara and Green Tara are, in essence, the same figure. They both represent the quintessence of compassion. I myself medi-tated upon Green Tara for nine years, and then took up White Tara. In doing so I felt the external forms change, and there were some differences of emphasis, but there was no essential change. Tara is Tara.

Apart from White Tara's additional function as bestower of long life, the two practices do have a different feel to them. Green Tara, with her right leg stepping down into the world, stresses the activity of compassion – like the spontaneous re-sponse of a mother to her child. White Tara sits in the vajra pos-ture, still extraordinarily compassionate, but more centred, more still. These differences are reflected in the fact that while Green Tara is often associated with the green Buddha Amogha-siddhi and his outward-going wisdom of infallible success,[12] White Tara is always regarded as belonging to the Lotus family of Amitabha, who could be characterized as the Buddha of meditation.[13]

The other striking difference between the two figures is that White Tara is adorned with seven eyes. She is that form of Tara that emphasizes that compassion must be wise. 'Fools rush in', but to help effectively you need to see clearly, to understand what is happening. White Tara's seven eyes communicate that, to be fully effective, compassion must spring from awareness, from a balanced attitude, and ultimately from wisdom. So the feeling of the meditation is stiller, more contemplative, than that of the more active Green Tara.

## Red Tara: Bringing Forth Natural Awareness

Another form of Tara, less commonly found in Tibetan Buddhist practice than the Green and White forms, is Red Tara.[14] While the common Tibetan name for Tara is Drolma, this form is called Rigjed Lhamo, which could be translated as 'the goddess who brings forth one's own natural awareness'. Meditation on this form of Tara aims to bring about a state of pure, non-dual awareness, which is said to be the mind in its natural simplicity.

The traditional texts say that the most effective times of day for performing this meditation are those when the sky may itself be red, i.e., sunrise and sunset. Red Tara is visualized, as are all these Buddhist deities, appearing in the midst of boundless blue sky. Her body is a brilliant ruby red in colour. Like most forms of Tara she appears as a young princess, dressed in the jewels and silks of a Bodhisattva.

Red Tara's figure is the same in its posture as Green Tara: she is seated with her left leg drawn up in meditation, and her right extended, as if stepping down into the world to help living beings. Her right hand is in the gesture of supreme generosity; her left in the gesture of bestowing the protection of the Three Jewels. Her long black hair is partly drawn up into a topknot, the rest cascading down over her shoulders.

However, as well as the wonderful warmth of her ruby red colour, there are other features that distinguish her from Green Tara. She is seated on a red lotus throne on which is a sun disc. Her right, gift-bestowing hand holds a vase of the nectar of immortality. Rather than blue lotuses, in her left hand she holds the stem of a red lotus that blossoms by her ear, on which rest a drawn bow and arrow, both made of small lotus flowers. She has a third eye in her forehead: a higher, wisdom eye.[15] Behind her is an aura of the full moon, and her body gives off light of the five colours associated with the wisdoms of the Five Buddhas, whom we shall meet in Chapter 4. Her mantra also differs from the usual ten-syllable Tara mantra, having only six syllables.

This red form of Tara is said to be particularly characterized by bounteousness and generosity. The vase of nectar that she holds shows that, like White Tara, she bestows longevity on her devotees. The flowery bow and arrow that rest on the lotus by her left shoulder are associated with the Indian god of love, Kamadeva, half-brother to Cupid, and just as good a shot. This suggests that Red Tara causes people to fall in love with the Dharma. If we are to go far on the spiritual path, we shall need to get our emotions strongly involved with the Dharma, otherwise, however much we may agree with Buddhist ideas and ideals, we shall not be able to engage much energy in them. Red Tara's brilliant colour suggests total emotional arousal, even passion. She causes people to love truth and freedom, wisdom and compassion, so passionately that they will do whatever it takes to embrace them. If you meditate on her beautiful form, she will attract you and draw you on, leading you ever more deeply into the heart of reality. As a result, you will eventually enter the realm of pure natural awareness, and Red Tara will have lived up to her Tibetan name.

## Yellow Tara: a Harvest of Good Qualities

Yet another form of Tara is Yellow Tara. Each of these colours seen in meditation – whether green, white, red, or yellow – is brilliant and vivid. It is sometimes the colour of the visualized figure that has the deepest impact on the meditator. On this level of inner experience, these pure colours themselves take on symbolic meaning. So Yellow Tara symbolically embodies all the qualities of things associated with golden yellow, especially grain and gold. Both are forms of riches, so for the Buddhist

Tantra yellow is especially the colour of wealth and increase. Although these Tantric meditations were often employed for worldly ends, so that Tara might be invoked for the sake of increasing wealth, Buddhism is fundamentally always concerned with Enlightenment. So this magic of increase came to be used for increasing all good qualities such as peace, energy, wisdom, and loving-kindness.

These Tantric meditations on yellow figures became a kind of harvest magic. The meditator used the ritual form of the meditation to convey a message to the depths of his or her mind. Under the inner sun of Yellow Tara's influence, abundant crops of positive qualities were encouraged to grow and flourish in all directions, until one day the meditator could harvest them and become like Yellow Tara, and go on to promote the spiritual growth of everyone with whom they came into contact.

The most common form of Yellow Tara has six arms. This may seem a little odd to us to start with, but Buddhist Tantric figures often have more arms, legs, or faces than are possible on the human plane. After all, we are dealing here with deep symbolism, not human anatomy. We have already seen White Tara, with her seven loving eyes. Additional arms represent the capacity to reach out in many directions at once to help living beings. Yellow Tara's principal right hand, like the other forms of Tara we have seen, is at her right knee, her palm turned outwards in a gesture of supreme generosity. Her main left hand is in her lap, holding a vase. Two of her other four hands hold symbols derived from the earth. One of her left hands holds a sheaf of grain. And one of her right hands holds a threefold jewel. Like Green Tara, she sits with her left leg drawn up in meditation, while her right is extended as if she is prepared at any moment to step down into the world.

Not surprisingly, given her symbolic associations, Yellow Tara is connected with the Earth Goddess (Vasundharā in Sanskrit).

The Earth Goddess makes a very important appearance in symbolic accounts of the historical Buddha's Enlightenment. To start with, accounts of the Buddha's Enlightenment described his experiences in terms of what he had understood, and the state of consciousness he had attained. As time went on, these descriptions did not seem to do justice to what had happened. So accounts started to appear that described the Buddha's Enlightenment in dramatic and symbolic terms. These were not less true than the more rational accounts. Enlightenment is an event that transforms your consciousness on all levels – from the rational to the very depths of what was the unconscious mind (for with Enlightenment the light of awareness permeates every aspect of the psyche, and nothing is left skulking in the shadows beyond it). These symbolic accounts then tell the story more as it would have been experienced on deeper, more non-rational levels of the Buddha's mind.

At that depth of consciousness, the Buddha's struggle for Enlightenment seems to have been experienced as a kind of cosmic drama, with the fate of the universe at stake. At one dramatic point Mara, who embodies everything that holds us back from awakening to the truth, approached the Buddha-to-be, and asked him a question: 'You have seated yourself on the diamond seat, the place where all the previous Buddhas have gained Enlightenment. By what right do you sit there?' This is a question that all Buddhists are likely to ask themselves at one time or another: 'What is so special about me? Who am I to be thinking about developing qualities like wisdom and compassion?' The Buddhist answer to us is that all life has the potential to grow in the direction of Enlightenment. The fact that we have become aware of that potential and begun to actualize it would be explained by Buddhism in terms of karma – that our positive actions in the past have developed in us a capacity to respond to the Dharma, to the call of freedom.

This, in effect was the Buddha's answer. He did not engage with Mara directly. He did not speak to him. He remained seated in meditation posture. But with the fingers of his right hand he touched the earth. The Earth Goddess instantly responded to this call, and appeared. Naturally, she sees everything that happens in her domain. So she was able to testify on behalf of the Buddha. She said she had witnessed endless past lives of the Buddha in which he had practised all kinds of good actions. It was because of all these good deeds that he could now sit by right on the diamond throne in order to gain Enlightenment. Thus here the Earth Goddess represents the aspect of the Buddha's mind that knew that the time was ripe for gaining Enlightenment, that he was ready to harvest the positive results of all the work he has done over endless lifetimes. So with the aid of the Earth Goddess, Mara's challenge was answered, and the Buddha gained his freedom.

Yellow Tara is said to bestow all kinds of riches, both worldly and spiritual. With her gesture of supreme giving she offers seven kinds of prosperity: mundane wealth, positive qualities, children, long life, happiness, praise, and wisdom.

## The Twenty-One Taras and their Praises

As Tara became a much-loved figure in India and Tibet, many devotional verses were written in her praise. Perhaps the most famous of these, whose eight-syllable lines are known by heart and chanted every day by many ordinary Tibetans, is the 'Homage to the Twenty-One Taras'. This set of verses is included in an Indian Tantra, 'Tara's Tantra: the Origin of all Rites', which was translated into Tibetan in the late twelfth century. The set includes an introductory verse, a set of twenty-one praises, and some verses at the end that describe the benefits to be gained from chanting the Homage with devotion to Tara. These include both mundane advantages, such as gaining wealth or curing infertility, and spiritual achievements, such as gaining complete fearlessness and making rapid progress in attaining Enlightenment.

The verses praise a number of different forms of Tara, though it is by no means clear that each of the twenty-one main verses is intended to express devotion to a different form. However, that is the tradition that has become established over time. So nowadays in Tibetan Buddhism the tradition is that you visualize in the sky in front of you a set of twenty-one forms of Tara, and then recite the verses with concentrated devotion to them.

There are actually three different traditions of visualizing and depicting the Twenty-One Taras. In one, the Taras are all shown in the iconographic form of Green Tara, but in various colours, and each holding a vase of a particular colour in their right hand. In a second, they are also in the Green Tara form, but again of various colours; this time, though, they have different emblems on the lotuses that they hold in their left hands. The third tradition presents the Taras in much more individualized forms, some standing, some seated, holding many different emblems. This third set, which might seem the most interesting, happens to be much less practised than the other two.[16]

Thus in Tibetan monasteries everywhere, and by pious lay people in front of their personal shrines, every day twenty-one beautiful, graceful forms of Tara are invoked, and when their shining presence has been established, the praise begins:

*Homage, Tārā, quick one, heroine,*
*whose eyes flash like lightning,*
*born from the opening corolla*
*of the lotus face of the Lord of the triple world.*

*Homage, Lady whose face is filled*
*with a hundred autumn moons,*
*blazing with the laughing beams*
*of the hosts of a thousand stars....*[17]

## The Goddess of the White Parasol

Having been born from the tears of Avalokita, the male Bodhi-sattva of Compassion, over time Tara took on many of his functions. A well-known form of Avalokita has a thousand arms, symbolizing the heartfelt desire of the Bodhisattva to reach out and rescue all living beings from suffering. As time went on, a female equivalent of this figure appeared. This unusual form of Tara is the Goddess of the White Parasol (Sitatapatra in Sanskrit). She is represented as a white goddess with not only a thousand arms but also a thousand heads of several different colours, and a thousand legs. Each face has a third eye, as does the palm of each hand and the sole of each foot. All her left hands hold arrows, and all her right hands hold wheels of the Dharma. Under her flowing skirt, her feet hold down a mass of figures and other things – symbolizing her capacity to protect her devotees from all harm, both spiritual and mundane.

In her main left hand she holds the handle of the white parasol from which she derives her name. The parasol is the first of the eight symbols of good fortune found in Buddhist tradition.[18] It is sometimes carried in processions of important lamas in Tibet. In that situation, it is made of white, yellow, or multi-coloured silk, and is large enough for four or five people to shelter under. Naturally a parasol has the function of protecting from the elements, particularly from the sun. In India, possessing an ornate parasol, particularly if it was held over you by a servant, was a symbol of power and wealth. Transferred onto a higher level, the parasol thus becomes a symbol of both spiritual protection and spiritual power. In particular it is said to protect from states of mind clouded by hatred, craving, pride, envy, or ignorance.

Representations of this figure are quite an artistic tour de force. Usually the goddess's multi-coloured heads are depicted arranged in rows, one above the other. Though the figure may seem a little odd to Western eyes, as we tend to read these things rather literally, as usual we are dealing here with symbolic truth. If we take the figure as the visual expression of the heartfelt desire that no one and nothing should ever suffer, and to do everything one can to be vigilant in this task, to reach out and help, and to shelter all beings from harm, then its true inner beauty is revealed. This deity is particularly popular with the Gelug school of Tibetan Buddhism, to which the Dalai Lama belongs.

## Vijaya

Lastly in this chapter we shall look at Vijaya, who is not thought of as a form of Tara, but who is often depicted with her.[19] She is a figure who forms part of a very popular triad of long-life deities in Tibetan Buddhism, together with White Tara and the Buddha Amitayus (a red Buddha holding a vase of immortality, whose name means 'boundless life'). Vijaya means victory. Vijaya is considered an emanation of the Buddha Vairocana, the white Buddha whose name means 'the illuminator'. White is the colour of purity, and her practice is believed to be very effective for purifying faults and hindrances as well as for gaining long life.

Vijaya appears in different forms, but is most commonly visualized as a white goddess with three faces and eight arms. Her central face is white, with a smiling expression, her right face (the one to your left as you are looking at her) is yellow, and her left face is blue and somewhat wrathful. Each face has three eyes.

With her main right hand she holds to her heart a multi-coloured crossed vajra – a symbolic diamond thunderbolt that we shall learn more about in the next chapter. Above this, with her main left hand she makes a gesture of warding off obstacles and hindrances, while clasping a noose – symbolic of binding all hindering forces. Her second right hand holds a small figure of the red Buddha Amitabha, seated on a lotus. The third holds an arrow, and the fourth is turned outwards at her knee in the gesture of supreme generosity. Her second left hand holds a bow. The third is raised above it in the gesture of bestowing the protection of the Three Jewels. The fourth rests in her lap, holding a vase of the nectar of immortality. She is dressed in jewels and silks, and her body is made of pure white light and surrounded by a white aura.

Vijaya is sometimes visualized seated in a stupa – a symbolic monument.[20] This suggests that she is an emanation of the Enlightened mind. She is attended by Avalokita and Vajrapani (the Bodhisattva who embodies spiritual energy), as well as other figures. Also, in a set of sadhanas, or meditation practices, known as the *Vajravali*, she is described seated in the middle of a mandala, a sacred circle, surrounded by thirty-two other figures.

# 3

## PERFECT WISDOM:
## THE BOOK THAT BECAME A GODDESS

### The Goddess of Perfect Wisdom

The two central qualities of Enlightenment are wisdom and compassion. Although she helps her devotees to develop both qualities quickly, Tara especially embodies compassion. So now it is time to look at the other side of the coin and meet a wisdom goddess. The figure of the Goddess of Perfect Wisdom first appeared in India around 300–500 CE, and over the centuries she assumed many different forms.[21] Since in Buddhist Tantra one mental picture is worth at least a thousand words, we'll start by seeing one of her most common forms in our mind's eye.

This form of the Wisdom Goddess is a brilliant golden yellow. She is seated cross-legged on a blue lotus and white moon mat. Her hands are held in the gesture of teaching the Dharma. She holds the stems of two lotuses, which open out into a pale blue blossom at each shoulder. On each of these is a white moon mat. On each moon mat lies a book of the Perfection of Wisdom. She wears a tiara with jewels of the colours of the Five Buddhas.

The Wisdom Goddess is visualized as a mature woman – though still very beautiful. Wisdom is something that takes time to ripen. The goddess is often described as 'the mother of all the Buddhas'. This is because she represents the realization of transcendental wisdom that sees unerringly the true nature of all things, and there is no other way to gain Enlightenment. It is only Perfect Wisdom that gives birth to Buddhahood. The goddess has given birth to countless Buddhas. She is said to regard the Buddhas like a mother fondly watching her children at play.

There is one particularly striking feature of the goddess. I have said that she is golden yellow, but if we look closely we shall see that the golden yellow light from her body is given off by millions of Buddhas. Her whole body is made up of golden Buddhas. It is as though the goddess of the Perfection of Wisdom is a great galaxy. Seen from afar the galaxy is in the most pleasing shape imaginable. Coming closer, we see that it comprises endless constellations of Buddhas, starry multitudes of people who have perfectly awakened to the true nature of things.

But before there was the Wisdom Goddess, there was the Perfection of Wisdom literature. The goddess and the texts are inextricably linked, one symbolizing wisdom in all its beauty, the other encapsulating – as far as is possible – the experience of Enlightenment. But why the shift? The fact is that gaining wisdom is at least as much a matter of becoming emotionally receptive as of intellectual sharpness. Thus the Perfection of Wisdom literature transformed itself into a goddess – to teach more effectively by appearing in a form that people would love to dwell upon.

## The Perfection of Wisdom Literature

According to tradition, the Perfection of Wisdom literature springs from Shakyamuni, the historical Buddha. He found that these teachings were not appropriate for the men and women of his time, so shortly before he died he entrusted the teachings to the *nagas*, traditional creatures who, in Buddhism, have something of the same characteristics as dragons in the West. They are long-lived, wise, and can function as guardians of treasures.

If we are to begin to enter into a proper relationship with these precious texts, we shall need to develop a feeling of appreciation, even of reverence, for the power of words. We have gained most of our knowledge through words, so even ordinary books can be precious. Books containing the highest insights of humanity must be extraordinary treasures indeed. *How* you read the Perfection of Wisdom literature is supremely important. One of the earliest Wisdom texts encourages us in its opening line to, 'Call forth as much as you can of love, of respect and of faith!'[22]

Although the Perfection of Wisdom literature uses words, it does so in order to help you to enter a realm in which words are transcended. The books themselves are just catalysts for a new vision of the universe. If you enter fully into that vision, an undreamed of realm begins to unfold itself. Then words will fail you. You will be unable to describe what you have seen and understood. Someone who has used the Perfection of Wisdom literature to enter that transcendental realm is said to be like a mute who has had a dream but has no way of communicating it.

## The Development of the Perfection of Wisdom Literature

The first Perfection of Wisdom teachings started to appear about 100 BCE and the basic texts of the literature appeared during a two-hundred-year phase of development. According to tradition they were given by the nagas to the great Indian Buddhist teacher Nagarjuna. In the two hundred years after the Perfection of Wisdom literature first appeared, it achieved great popularity. So much devotion was lavished upon it that it expanded. One text even reached 100,000 lines in length.

The succeeding two hundred years (roughly 300–500 CE) saw the Perfection of Wisdom spread throughout India and into China. In this phase the new texts became increasingly concise. Among them are two of the most famous and important of all Buddhist works: the *Diamond Sutra* and the *Heart Sutra*.

During this period, too, something very remarkable happened. The Perfection of Wisdom, under the influence of the Tantra, began to change. This literature of uncompromising paradox and intellectual subtlety transformed itself. From being an intellectual thunderbolt, destroying conceptualizations, it was reborn as a wisdom goddess and a mantra. Examining this extraordinary development can give us insights into the Tantric approach to self-transformation.

Buddhist Tantra is always concerned with direct experience. Rather than using lots of words and concepts to give you an idea of what reality is like, it employs a completely different approach. It tries to help you leave behind words and concepts *about* reality, and to experience it directly. It encourages you to do this by entering an imaginative realm. You enter a realm of light, travel in a realm of gold. In this archetypal realm you are brought face to face with Wisdom, in the most appealing form imaginable.

Devotion to the Goddess of Perfect Wisdom spread, over time, to Japan, Java, Cambodia, China, and Tibet, though the Tibetans had already fallen in love with Tara, whom we have already met, so her cult never gained great popularity there. It was in India, above all, that the goddess manifested. There was even a great statue of her on the Vulture's Peak at Rajgir, where the Buddha had given many discourses. She appeared in many different forms: sometimes golden, sometimes white. She could have two, four, or six arms, or even (in a form that became popular in Cambodia) eleven heads and eleven pairs of arms.

India being the centre of devotion to the goddess, when the Muslims trampled Buddhism underfoot in that country, her cult largely disappeared. As the Muslims systematically destroyed the monasteries, smashed statues, and burned books, the Wisdom Goddess went into hiding. It is really only in the twentieth century, and largely due to the work of one man, that the goddess is once again displaying her face in so many different lands. The life's work of the German scholar Edward Conze was to translate virtually all the Perfection of Wisdom texts into English. Thanks to his efforts the goddess once more moves freely among us.

## Emblems of the Wisdom Goddess

In her different manifestations, the Goddess of Perfect Wisdom is shown with various symbols or emblems. There are six main ones, and it will help us to understand the Wisdom Goddess better if we look briefly at each of them in turn.

Firstly there is the lotus, which is a symbol for what transcends the mundane: for what grows out of the mud of confusion and unawareness, rises up through the clear water of higher states of consciousness, and finally emerges into the sunlight of wisdom. So although we have been speaking of her as a goddess and of meeting her in the archetypal realm, it is clear that she is essentially a manifestation of reality itself.

The lotus is also a symbol of spiritual receptivity. To 'understand' the Perfection of Wisdom we have to be prepared to stand under it and learn from it. In doing so we may even have to accept that we do not know anything about anything, spiritual or mundane! This is, in a sense, the message of the *Heart Sutra* – that our experience is ungraspable, and even the concepts of Buddhism do not capture the truth of things. The traditional image for this is that verbal explanations are like fingers pointing to the moon. When someone points to the moon, you look at the sky, not at their finger. But often, in spiritual matters, we tend to go from one explanation to the next, and never see what the whole thing is pointing to.

Her association with the next symbol, the book, emphasizes that she embodies the wisdom of all the books in the Perfect Wisdom literature. The book also represents the fact that although we aspire to go beyond words and concepts, most of us cannot just ignore culture and learning. An irrational, 'I just want to get out of my head' approach does not usually work. Like it or not, most of us think more or less continuously throughout the day. We shall do better to train and clarify our rational faculty rather than try to ignore it. We can let it take us as far on the spiritual path as it can, and then make the fathomless leap beyond it, into the realm of the Perfection of Wisdom.

The next symbol is the vajra. This is a symbolic sceptre, said to have all the immutable qualities of the diamond, and all the destructive power of a thunderbolt. It may seem strange for a gentle goddess to wield such a weapon – though Athena, the wisdom goddess of ancient Greece, is also a warrior. Transcendental wisdom is both soft and hard. It is soft in the sense that it is subtle and elusive. If you try to grasp it directly you will always fail. It comes to you gently, from the side, as it were – from a 'direction' you cannot cover. It is hard in the sense that it smashes to pieces all our mundane ideas about reality. Thus Perfect Wisdom has a destructive aspect, which the diamond thunderbolt well symbolizes.

The flaming sword, the next of her emblems, has a vajra handle, a double-edged blade, and flames dancing at its tip. The goddess shares this emblem with Manjushri – the male Bodhi-

VAJRA

sattva of Wisdom. Manjushri and the Perfect Wisdom goddess represent two methods of approach to the goal of wisdom, so it is not surprising that they should share certain symbols.

A *mala* is what in the West would be called a rosary.[23] In Buddhism it is used for counting mantras and other practices. Its association with the goddess suggests the importance of repetition for arriving at wisdom. In the West especially, where Novelty is the great goddess, we tend to flit from one experience to another. All too often, having done or read something once, or at most a few times, we feel we have drunk the experience to the dregs. Novelty lives on the surface of life, but Perfect Wisdom is preserved in the depths.

To achieve wisdom through the Perfection of Wisdom texts we need to read them repeatedly. (Some of the sutras reiterate their message – eighty per cent of the *Perfection of Wisdom in 100,000 Lines* consists of repetitions.) We need to meditate repeatedly on the wisdom that they contain. It is only with this devoted, loving return to the same sources of inspiration that we shall gradually deepen our insight into reality, and come to understand the same texts and subjects in ever-deepening ways. The goddess does not reveal all her secrets at a first meeting. To woo her successfully we have to be faithful to her.

Lastly there is the begging-bowl. This is the utensil of the wanderer, the monk or nun. It symbolizes the movement away from worldly ties. It implies the need for renunciation if we are to find Perfect Wisdom. We may not physically leave our home and our country, but in the search for Wisdom we shall have to be prepared to give up our old cramped self and our conventional ideas about the world.

## Perfect Wisdom in Symbolic Sound

When you are meditating on the Perfect Wisdom goddess, at a certain point after you have visualized her, light emanates from the centre of the galaxy, from the heart of the goddess. Down the light ray comes her mantra: *om ah dhih hum svaha*. It enters your heart and begins to echo there, bestowing wisdom on you through another of its transformations.

The mantra *om ah dhih hum svaha* conveys the message of the Perfection of Wisdom literature, but through the medium of symbolic sound. It is one of three mantras commonly associated with the Perfection of Wisdom. It is not readily translatable, appealing only to a level of the mind that does not trade in words. The other two common mantras can be given some rational explanation.

Firstly there is the mantra *gate gate paragate parasamgate bodhi svaha*. This comes at the end of the *Heart Sutra*, and is more generally associated with the Perfection of Wisdom literature than with the Wisdom Goddess, though it does appear in some of her meditation practices. It has been translated by Edward Conze as 'Gone, gone, gone beyond, gone altogether beyond, O what an awakening, all hail!'[24]

The mantra symbolizes a deepening understanding of reality. According to one tradition its first four words correspond to the four levels of emptiness. The emptiness (*shunyata* in Sanskrit) of oneself and all things is a central idea in Buddhism, a key to understanding the nature of wisdom, yet it is a concept that is easy to misunderstand. Essentially it means that nothing exists by or of itself. All things are empty of anything fixed, any unchanging core. So Buddhist wisdom sees everything in terms of energy, as dynamic processes of constant change depending on conditions. All phenomena are momentary, constantly transforming. That applies to us as well. We tend always to have a sense of a fixed 'I' or 'me' that somehow stands above and apart from the flow of our lives. Most of our lives are in fact spent in preserving and guarding this 'I' from danger, keeping it secure and comfortable. Yet, strangely enough, when we try to find it or pin it down, we discover we cannot do so. This is because a fixed 'I' unaffected by conditions does not exist, or, to put it in traditional Buddhist language, all things are empty of an inherently-existing self.

Understanding this emptiness, which is a quality of all phenomena, from atoms to galaxies, and all life, from amoebas to us humans, is what enables us to meet with the Goddess of Perfect Wisdom. However, it is easy to misunderstand what Buddhism means by 'emptiness'. Our minds have a tendency to turn concepts into things. Emptiness is a useful way of describing a quality that all things have – they are all dynamic processes, devoid of anything fixed and unchangeable. But it is easy to turn this empty quality of phenomena into some kind of a thing – to start imagining that things have a true nature called emptiness. If we do that we are back in a world of fixed ideas once again, and we have inadvertently turned our back on the Wisdom Goddess. Life is always in motion, and we become most alive when we let go of all our fixed ideas about it.

In the mantra, the first *gate* (pronounced roughly like 'guttay') symbolizes going beyond samsara. As we have seen, samsara is mundane existence, which is characterized by the fact that, although it can be happy and pleasurable at times, it never finally satisfies us. Indeed it is often very painful, as it inevitably involves the sufferings of being born, getting ill, growing old and dying, as well as being separated from things that we like, being saddled with things that we dislike, and often not getting what we want. For Buddhism, which believes in rebirth, mundane existence is a round of seemingly-endless unsatisfactoriness that we can only escape by gaining nirvana, or Enlightenment.

The second *gate* represents the emptiness of nirvana, of Enlightenment itself. This does not mean that there is no such thing as Enlightenment. Firstly it means that Enlightenment is devoid of the qualities of samsara. Samsara was unsatisfactory. Nirvana is totally and permanently satisfying. It has the totally fulfilling qualities that we have spent forever trying unsuccessfully to wring out of mundane life. Secondly it suggests that Enlightenment is not something we can adequately describe in words and concepts. Nirvana is an experience we can come to taste if we make the effort to do so, but it is likely to turn out to be different from what we imagined. In particular, people often view Enlightenment as a kind of heaven world, somehow distinct or separate from the phenomenal world. This second *gate* denies all our ideas and expectations about what Enlightenment is like, which often get in the way of actually experiencing it.

With *paragate* you realize the emptiness of all distinctions, and in particular that between samsara and nirvana. Samsara and nirvana are not like two different countries; they are two ways of approaching life, two ways in which we use our minds. Nirvana is samsara seen with love and wisdom. Samsara is nirvana muddied with hatred, craving, and confusion.

Lastly, with *parasamgate* you see the emptiness of all concepts whatsoever. You recognize that life can never be caught in words. Ideas are very useful and necessary for helping us to stand back and understand the nature of reality, but once they

*Plate One (previous page)* GREEN TARA
*Plate Two* WHITE TARA
*Plate Three (opposite)* VIJAYA

*Plate Four* PRAJNAPARAMITA

*Plate Five* PRAJNAPARAMITA (DETAIL)

*Plate Six* VAJRAVARAHI

*Plate Seven* MACHIK LABDRON
*Plate Eight (overleaf)* KUAN YIN

have helped us to do so we need to let them go. It is like using road signs to drive to a city you have never visited: the road signs help you to see which way you need to go, but you just read them and drive on; you do not pull them up and put them in the back of the car once they have pointed you on your way. Finally, as concepts drop away and you experience life directly as it really is, even the idea of emptiness itself will have done its job. You will need to let that drop too.

The other phrase which can be repeated as a mantra is the homage found at the beginning of the *Heart Sutra: om namo bhagavatyai aryaprajnaparamitayai.* Edward Conze translates this as 'Homage to the Perfection of Wisdom, the Lovely, the Holy'.[25] The *gate gate* mantra, with its association with the four levels of shunyata, might appeal to those more intellectually inclined, whereas this invocation is an outpouring of faith and devotion to the goddess. It is characteristic of Buddhism that it should provide such differing paths to the goal of Enlightenment.

## Benefits of Meditating on the Perfect Wisdom Goddess

Regular meditation on the Wisdom Goddess produces an ever-deepening involvement with her. Her beautiful golden figure is a compelling focus for devotion. For men, her visualization can often absorb the romantic and other feelings that might be evoked by meeting a beautiful, mature woman. For women she is a figure with whom to identify, the most positive of all role models. Thus for both sexes energy can easily be engaged by the meditation, and so poured into the contemplation of Wisdom.

If this process continues, the practice enters the realm of the archetypal. In Jungian terms, a man may project the highest aspect of his anima, while a woman may encounter the Magna

Mater – the Great Mother. She becomes for the meditator the archetypal Wisdom Goddess found in many traditions. For the Gnostics she was Sophia, for the Greeks, Athena. She is found in the Tarot as the High Priestess, wearing a headdress of the crescent moon, and holding a scroll – corresponding to the book of the Perfection of Wisdom. She is seated between two pillars – one light, one dark. Imbibing her knowledge will enable you to pass between the pillars and transcend all dualistic thinking.

In India, the Wisdom Goddess assumed the form we have seen – once described as staggeringly beautiful to the point of being scorching. Her meditation can become a way of experiencing the archetypal beauty of the refined levels of one's mind. Finally, with faithful practice, it can become far more than that. The goddess can introduce us to the experience of transcendental wisdom itself – the transcendence of the world of subject and object.

*Homage to you, Perfect Wisdom,*
*Boundless, and transcending thought!*
*All your limbs are without blemish,*
*Faultless those who you discern.*

*Spotless, unobstructed, silent,*
*Like the vast expanse of space;*
*Who in truth does really see you*
*The Tathāgata perceives.*[26]

# 4

## THE CONSORTS OF THE FIVE BUDDHAS AND THEIR MANDALA

### Sexual Symbolism in Tantric Buddhism

As Tantric Buddhism developed in India, its richness and abundance expressed itself in thousands of different figures. Thankfully, this great mass of figures can be organized into certain characteristic patterns. Perhaps the most well-known and important way of patterning Tantric deities is the mandala of the Five Buddhas, also known as the Vajradhatu mandala – the mandala of the sphere of the diamond thunderbolt. These five archetypal Buddhas came to be seen as the heads of five families, into which nearly all Tantric deities could be arranged. So, for instance, we have already seen that White Tara is associated with the Lotus family of the red Buddha, Amitabha. More than that, the Five Buddhas came to be symbolically associated with many other things, such as a time of day, a direction of the compass, a symbolic animal, and so on. In this way almost every aspect of life could be associated with one of these five figures, and therefore with an aspect of Enlightenment.

As time went on, the Five Buddhas came to be represented seated in sexual embrace with female consorts. These *yab-yum* (a Tibetan honorific phrase meaning father-mother) couples are regarded with particular veneration by Vajrayana devotees, as expressions of the highest truth. Yab-yum forms probably developed for several reasons. They expressed the increasing importance being given to the feminine principle in Tantric Buddhism; they enabled the deep and powerful energies associated with sex to be incorporated into the quest for Enlightenment; most important of all, they provided a way of symbolizing, in very vivid form, the mystery of what is called *yuganaddha* ('two-in-oneness'). The aim of Tantric Buddhism is to produce states of Enlightened consciousness in which different characteristics of reality are experienced together. In such states, wisdom and compassion become inseparable, so do bliss and emptiness – the experience of the ungraspable nature of reality.

Thus when we see representations of these yab-yum couples, we need to understand that they are really two aspects of one figure. In a yab-yum figure, the female represents the wisdom aspect of the Enlightened experience, so she is often referred to as the *prajna*, or wisdom, of the Buddha. The male symbolizes the method or skilful means through which that wisdom is compassionately expressed in the world. The female aspects of these yab-yum figures each communicate a particular aspect of the wisdom of Enlightenment.

Let us now meet the consorts of the Five Buddhas. To do this, we need in our mind's eye to enter their mandala – the sacred circle of figures, usually represented as being within a beautiful palace adorned with precious things. Different Buddhist Tantric texts vary in assigning some of the consorts to different Buddhas, and their symbolic associations also differ. But here we shall follow the arrangement that is given in the well-known text which in the West we call the *Tibetan Book of the Dead*. So if we enter the mandala palace from the east, we shall first see the blue figure of Locana, embraced by the deep blue Buddha Akshobhya. Locana means 'she with the eye'. She expresses the clear seeing of the 'mirror-like wisdom'. When you experience this wisdom, your mind reflects everything perfectly clearly, without any subjective distortions. Like a mirror and its reflections, your mind does not cling to or avoid any experience. As it is not pulled or pushed by craving or aversion, it becomes absolutely still, calm, and unwavering.

If we now move round the mandala into the south, we see the yellow Mamaki, embraced by the Buddha Ratnasambhava. Mamaki means 'mine maker' – she feels for all living beings as though they were her own children, her own self. They are all hers. She feels as though the whole universe is hers. When you possess her wisdom you think of everything as 'mine'. When everything is yours, when you feel for everyone, then is born the 'wisdom of equality' that is particularly associated with Mamaki. This wisdom sees the common factors in all experience. It sees that it is all empty of any inherently-existing selfhood. All things are just appearances to the mind; they arise and disappear as conditions change. Everything, all forms of life, all experiences, are the same in the sense that they are open-ended, constantly transforming into something else.

Moving on to the western side of the mandala, we see the red figure of Pandaravasini ('white-robed one'), embraced by the ruby-red Buddha Amitabha. Pandaravasini is sometimes said to be a form of White Tara. Her white robe also suggests the simile given by the Buddha in the Pali canon for the feelings of someone experiencing the fourth *dhyana*, or deep meditative absorption. In this state, the Buddha says, you are like someone who on a very hot day takes a cool bath, and then puts on a fresh white robe. White reflects the sun, and radiates light. Similarly, in the fourth dhyana your mind is so positive that its influence radiates and can even positively affect your environment and other people. So Pandaravasini perhaps expresses aspects of meditative experience – with which Amitabha is especially linked because his hands are in his lap, palms resting on one another, tips of the thumbs touching, in the dhyana, or meditation, mudra. In addition, she embodies the 'discriminating wisdom'. This wisdom gives the other side of the coin from the wisdom of equality, which saw what was common to all experience. The discriminating wisdom, on the other hand, sees all phenomena in their uniqueness. It experiences the way in which no two moments, no two experiences, are ever the same.

Going on to the northern side of the mandala, we find Green Tara, whom we have already met, with her consort, the deep green Buddha Amoghasiddhi. Her fearless compassion and instant response to the needs of living beings are expressions of her 'all-accomplishing wisdom'. This wisdom expresses the fact that your understandings are only fully mature when they become so natural, so integral to your being, that they affect all your actions. The all-accomplishing wisdom is knowing expressed through volitions. The highest volition is, of course, to act for the benefit of all living beings. When you reach a level at which you can act out of understanding the true nature of things, then you are able to accomplish infinite actions for the welfare of all that lives.

Finally, coming to the centre of the mandala, we enter the radiance of the pure white Akashadhatvishvari ('sovereign lady of the sphere of infinite space'), in union with the white Buddha Vairocana.[27] Here, the complementary nature of yab and yum is clearly shown. Vairocana, whose name means 'the illuminator', radiates the light of Buddhahood. Yet for light to radiate there must be space for it to pass through. Akashadhatvishvari represents the infinite space of Enlightened consciousness, which is illuminated by the brilliant wisdom of Enlightenment. She embodies the wisdom of the *dharmadhatu* – the sphere of the complete realization of the true nature of things. In this sphere, the light of wisdom and the space of emptiness dance together, united in one experience.

Sometimes, seeing representations of these yab-yum figures, people wonder why the male figures are represented as larger, facing the viewer, while their smaller female consort is clasped to their chest. It has to be said that sometimes things are the other way round, with female figures represented as the central figure of a mandala embracing a rather less individualized male consort. But generally it is the male figures that are given greater prominence. Doubtless this has to do with the history of Tantric Buddhism. Though there are women who play important roles in some of the Tantric practice lineages, one does gain the impression that the practices were mainly developed with male meditators in mind. Thus, apart from Tara and, to a much lesser extent, Locana, the consorts of the Five Buddhas are not so individualized, not developed so much as independent figures, as their male counterparts. It is quite unusual for the set of the five consorts to be represented as separate from the Five Buddhas – certainly when compared to the frequency with which the Five Buddhas are represented without their consorts.

In the West, where there are many women seriously practising the Dharma who are looking for models from which to draw inspiration, this situation is almost certain to change. I am sure these five figures, Locana and the rest, will eventually cease to draw their main significance from their relation to the Five Buddhas. They will become not so much consorts of the Buddhas, but the five prajnas (or wisdoms), a mandala of female Buddhas, standing alone, embodying all the qualities of Enlightenment within themselves.

## Queens of the Mandala

An attempt at allowing these five female Buddhas to express their qualities more fully appears in a cycle of sadhanas produced in the West, called 'Queens of the Mandala'. Some people may deny the validity of such new meditation practices, but it seems to me that the Dharma continues to unfold after 2,500 years, and it is a psychological and spiritual necessity for new expressions of Enlightenment to appear in response to changing cultural circumstances. Those figures that are either not relevant to people's spiritual needs, or that do not embody something of the 'taste of freedom' of Enlightenment, will disappear, or become museum pieces within the Buddhist tradition. Those that speak to contemporary Buddhist practitioners will flourish.

So let us briefly meet these five Queens of the Mandala, one by one. Again we can start in the east, where we see the beautiful figure of Locana – the embodiment of the mirror-like wisdom and the element water – seated on a pale blue lotus and a moon mat. She is blue in colour, seated in the vajra posture. She is dressed in exquisite clothing, and adorned with diamonds and other precious things. Her right hand is in the earth-touching mudra holding a golden vajra. Her left hand is at her heart. On its open palm stands a vajra-bell.

It is very unusual to see any Tantric figure holding a vajra-bell to their heart in this way. The male Buddha, Vajrasattva ('diamond being') is very commonly shown holding a vajra to his heart with his right hand. He is a very important Tantric deity, who is frequently meditated on in Tibetan Buddhism to help purify the mind. Vajrasattva is sometimes considered to be related to Akshobhya, Locana's consort, so it is interesting that she appears to be mirroring Vajrasattva. But while he holds the vajra to his heart with his right hand, emphasizing the masculine and compassionate method, Locana holds the bell to her heart with her left hand, emphasizing the feminine, and wisdom. The two gestures of Vajrasattva and Locana are mirror images, suggesting the mirror-like wisdom of which Locana is the serene embodiment.

On Locana's head is a five-jewelled crown. She has long black hair, some of which is bound up in a topknot, the rest flowing over her shoulders. In front of her topknot sits the deep-blue Buddha Akshobhya. He sits in the vajra posture, with his right hand in the earth-touching mudra, and his left resting in his lap, supporting an upright golden vajra. Locana's head and body are surrounded by auras of light. She is very beautiful, with calm blue eyes that take in everything.

If we now move round into the south of the mandala, we come upon Mamaki, who as we have seen embodies the wisdom of equality. She is also associated with the element earth. We see her seated on a pale yellow lotus on a moon mat. She is yellow in colour, seated in the relaxed posture known as royal ease. She is dressed in exquisite clothing, and adorned with an amber necklace and other ornaments made of gold and precious things. Her right hand is in the mudra of supreme giving, palm turned out by her right knee, and holds a wish-fulfilling gem. Her left hand is in front of her heart in the mudra of bestowing the protection of the Three Jewels. She is holding the stem of a pale blue lotus flower that blossoms at her left shoulder. On it is a moon mat, upon which stands a vajra-bell.

On her head is a five-jewelled crown. She has long black hair, some of which is bound in a topknot, the rest flowing over her shoulders. In front of her topknot sits the deep yellow Buddha Ratnasambhava. He sits in the vajra posture, his right hand in the mudra of supreme giving, and his left resting in his lap supporting a wish-fulfilling jewel.[28]

Mamaki's head and body are surrounded by auras of light. She is very beautiful, serene and relaxed. Her whole visualization

and symbolism suggest warmth and relaxation. This is appropriate as she is associated with the southern direction which (for
those of us who live in the northern hemisphere at least) is associated with the heat of the sun at noon. Yellow is the colour of
gold and riches, which here of course particularly means inner
riches – the riches of loving and wise states of mind. There is
nothing about her of the tightness of meanness, the tautness of
worrying if there is enough to share. Everything about her suggests expansiveness, and a sense that there are enough riches in
the universe for them to be shared with all beings. On the spiritual level this is true.

Mamaki's relaxedness springs also from her wisdom of equality. Our tension and anxiety all come from a sense of being separate, cut off from the rest of the world and other people. In this
state, we compare ourselves with others, thinking all the time in
terms of being superior, inferior, or equal to others. All these
comparisons are a source of suffering for us. Mamaki has put
them all down, and is completely relaxed and serene.

As we travel on into the west, we find Pandaravasini, 'the
white-robed', seated on a pale red lotus and a moon mat. She
embodies both the discriminating wisdom and the element fire.
Her body is brilliant red in colour, and she sits in the vajra posture. She is wearing exquisite clothing, of which at least the up-
per garment is pure white. She is adorned with rubies and other
precious things. Her hands are at her heart in the '*anjali*' mudra
of devotion. They hold the stems of two lotuses that blossom at
her shoulders. At her right shoulder is a red lotus on which, on a
moon mat, is a vase of immortality. At her left shoulder is a pale
blue lotus on which, on a moon mat, is a vajra-bell.

Why should Pandaravasini, who is a fully Enlightened female
Buddha, be displaying the mudra of devotion? We might think
this is a gesture that unenlightened people make, that you go beyond at a certain stage of the spiritual path. But that is not the

case. After his Enlightenment, the historical Buddha is said to have looked around for someone or something towards which he could express reverence and gratitude. As he could not see any human being who was his equal, he decided that he would express reverence for the truth he had discovered, the limitless mystery of consciousness he had fathomed. Faith is actually said to be a component of all positive mental states. In Buddhism this faith is not blind, but based on reason, experience, and spiritual intuition. So Pandaravasini reminds us that faith, devotion, reverence, and gratitude are important qualities at all stages of spiritual development. Her Lotus family is particularly associated with the 'heart' qualities of love and compassion, and also with communication, so it is she, rather than one of her Prajna sisters, who makes the mudra of devotion.

On her head is a five-jewelled crown. She has long black hair, some of which is bound up in a topknot, the rest flowing over her shoulders. In front of her topknot sits the deep red Buddha Amitabha. He is seated in the vajra posture. His right hand holds up a red lotus. His left rests in his lap, holding a setting sun.

Pandaravasini's head and body are surrounded by auras of light. She is very beautiful, smiling at you with infinite loving-kindness.

Entering the north of the mandala, we encounter Tara, whom we met in Chapter 2. She is represented here in a slightly different form, as she is related to the other female Buddhas around her. She embodies the all-accomplishing wisdom and is associated with the element air. She is seated on a pale blue lotus and a moon mat. Her body is green in colour. She sits with her left leg drawn up in meditation posture and her right leg extended, the foot resting on another small pale blue lotus and moon mat. She is dressed in exquisite clothing, and is adorned with silver and other precious things.

Her right hand is at her right knee, palm turned outwards in the mudra of supreme giving, holding a crossed vajra. Her left hand is in front of her heart, ringing a silver vajra-bell. This sounding of the vajra-bell relates to a number of the traditional associations made with the Karma family of which Green Tara is the prajna. We have seen that this family is associated with the element air, and therefore also with sound. Her consort, Amoghasiddhi, is pulled through the air by powerful birds, or bird-men, who clash cymbals as they fly. Much of the symbolism of this family is also associated with the union of opposites, suggested by the side-to-side movement of the bell as it rings. 'Karma' literally means 'action', so it is appropriate that Tara's left hand is in movement, while her right reaches outwards, to help all beings. The vajra-bell here functions almost as an alarm-bell, warning living beings of the peril of staying in samsara, and giving them a sense of the direction in which they can head in order to escape and find a safe refuge.

On Tara's head is a five-jewelled crown. She has long black hair, some of which is bound up into a topknot, the rest flowing over her shoulders. In front of her topknot sits the deep green Buddha, Amoghasiddhi. He is seated in the vajra posture. His right hand is in the *abhaya* mudra, the gesture of fearlessness; his left rests in his lap, holding a crescent moon.

Tara's head and body are surrounded by auras of light. She is young, beautiful, and smiling compassionately.

Finally we must come to the centre of the mandala, to meet Akashadhatvishvari, who embodies the wisdom of the dharmadhatu, the sphere of reality, and is associated with the element space. She sits on a white lotus and moon seat. Her body is brilliant white in colour. She sits with her legs crossed in the vajra posture. She is wearing exquisite clothing, and has adornments of sapphire and other precious things.

Her hands are at her heart, in the mudra of turning the Wheel of the Dharma. Between the thumb and forefinger of her right hand she holds the stem of a pale blue lotus that blossoms at her right shoulder. On the lotus is a white moon mat, on which stands a golden *dharmacakra*. This is a golden wheel whose eight spokes symbolize the Buddha's central teaching of the Noble Eightfold Path.[29] Her left hand also holds the stem of a pale blue lotus between her thumb and forefinger. This lotus blossoms at her left shoulder, supporting a moon mat, on which stands a silver vajra-bell.

On her head is a five-jewelled crown. She has long black hair, some of which is bound up into a topknot, the rest flowing over her shoulders. In front of her topknot sits the brilliant white Buddha Vairocana. He is seated in the vajra posture. His hands rest in his lap in dhyana mudra, holding a golden sun. Akashadhatvishvari's head and body are surrounded by auras of light. She is regal, intensely beautiful, serene and smiling.

All the symbolism associated with this family is of royalty, centrality, and light. Vairocana holds a sun, which forms the glowing centre of the solar system. Akashadhatvishvari also holds a *dharmacakra*. This is a solar symbol; in the inner world of the mind, it is the Dharma that lights up the darkness of ignorance, just as the sun gives light to the planets.

Whether these particular forms of Locana and the others will be taken to heart by Buddhist meditators remains to be seen. However, over the coming centuries, as Buddhism takes root in the West and Western views of the equality of the sexes impact on traditional Buddhism, it will be very surprising if we do not see these five female Buddhas stepping forward to become prominent figures in one beautiful form or another.

## Salutation to Locana

*Dawn of wisdom,*
*Your blue radiance illuminates*
*A new world, free from suffering.*
*Your eyes are calm oceans,*
*Reflecting perfection,*
*Seeing all, knowing all.*
*To you I joyfully prostrate.*

*Dawn of wisdom,*
*Your slender fingers*
*Touch the bedrock of reality,*
*Stroking the heads of the four great ghosts.*[30]
*Your upturned palm supports the vajra-bell,*
*The empty mandala of the Wisdom Goddess.*
*To you I reverently prostrate.*

*Dawn of wisdom,*
*Destroyer of all suffering,*
*In the vajra-sphere beyond subject and object*
*You fashion the jagged shards of hatred*
*Into wisdom's diamond adornments.*
*To you I lovingly prostrate.*

*Dawn of wisdom,*
*Vajra Queen,*
*Buddha from time before time,*
*Complete in yourself,*
*And consort of the noble Akshobhya.*
*To you I endlessly prostrate.*

# 5

## THE DAKINI: FREEDOM AND INSPIRATION

### Dancing in the Sky

A Tibetan yogi visited India many times searching for a highly-realized teacher who could show him the way to full Enlightenment. All the teachers he met told him that he should try to meet the yogini Niguma. On just hearing the name of Niguma, the yogi was filled with great happiness, and he set off to find her. He had been told that she had gone beyond any dependence on the physical body, but that she sometimes appeared in a certain cemetery.

When he arrived in the fearful cemetery, the yogi sat down fearlessly in the midst of corpses and wild animals. As a result, he had a vision of a brown woman dancing ecstatically in the sky high above his head. She was completely naked except for a few ornaments, all made of human bone. She carried a staff and a skull cup. Sometimes she multiplied herself into many wild dancing figures, filling the sky; at other times there was just one great figure in the air above him.

The yogi realized he must be in the presence of Niguma, and asked for instruction. But the wild dancing figure said she was an ogress, and when her helpers arrived they would feast on his blood; he had better escape while he still had his skin. He ignored this threat, and continued asking for teaching. Seeing he could not be scared away, Niguma changed tack. She asked him for a large amount of gold for her teaching. (In Buddhist Tantra it is usual to give something of value for initiation, to demonstrate one's seriousness, and out of gratitude for the immense spiritual riches to which the empowerment gives access.) The yogi had saved up a great deal of gold with which to seek teachings in India. Very reverently he offered it all to Niguma. Without a moment's hesitation she threw it away into the jungle.

If there had been any doubt in the yogi's mind before, it was wiped away by this evidence of the yogini's complete non-attachment, even to tremendous wealth. He knew he was dealing with an Enlightened teacher. Niguma then proceeded to give him initiation, much of it in dreams.

Niguma is a classic example of the kind of figure known in Buddhist tantra as a dakini. Personally, I think it is impossible to produce an adequate definition of what that word means. To try to catch a dakini in the iron trap of mundane logic is a hopeless task. In one Sanskrit dictionary the word is said to refer to a class of flesh-eating demoness. The Tibetan translation literally means female sky-goer. Sometimes she is referred to as a sky dancer. (The male counterparts, dakas, do exist, but they play a secondary role in the Tantra, whereas dakinis are central to it.)

To meet a dakini is not easy. They are not domesticated but wild. In fact you could say that the dakini is Enlightenment expressing itself through the archetype of the Wild Woman. Her wildness is not craziness, although some of her actions, born out of deep intuition, may be unfathomable to the part of us that always wants logical proof. She is wild because she lives in the wilderness, and rejoices in its vast freedom. This wilderness is not a place. You will not find it in the deserts of New Mexico or the empty heights of Tibet. (Though by a kind of Hermetic magic of 'as above, so below' dwelling in open places beyond the reach of civilization for a while may help us to contact the dakini's true realm.) The dakini erupts out of another realm of experience altogether. She lives at the end of the world, symbolized by her dancing in the sky, beyond the earth, unreachable. She lives beyond time. So Niguma appears in a cremation ground, the place where mundane life has run its course.

Fundamentally the wilderness in which the dakini delights is the vast space that is beyond the control of the ego. To find her you have to leave behind the security of your own views and ideas. You have to abandon the tidy civilized world of mundane concepts. You have to walk out into the unknown, the unexplored, the unimaginable.

In the cremation ground the bodies of all narrow, limiting ways of being are brought to be disposed of, to be reduced to powder. There we see that they were insubstantial. They had seemed so important, strutting their stuff, full of ideas and opinions, dos and don'ts. Now that the air has gone out of them, and the flames are taking hold, we see there was hardly anything there; they are just steam, bone, and ash. In particular, in the cremation ground, we may catch a glimpse of the fact that what we think of as 'I' or 'me' – the fixed unchanging self that goes through life and has experiences – is an illusion. When we see that clearly, we are free to leave the ground of mundane life, and to dance in the sky of infinite freedom.

As she is not fixed in any way, the dakini can appear anywhere, at any time – though paradoxically wherever she appears she never leaves the sky of emptiness. Not only can she turn up in many different circumstances, she is also quite capable of shifting shape. She may manifest as a beautiful young maiden or goddess, or as a decrepit old crone. She may appear as voluptuous and alluring, or as threatening. She is likely to appear ugly when she has been greatly neglected. If you have been living a life where everything revolves around and serves you, if you have mortgaged your life to the sensible and secure, if you have a sign at your front gate reading 'No poets, fire-eaters, tigers, or dwarves with golden eyes,' and if, despite all this, you have the good fortune to have a dakini come to your rescue, then however beautiful her real appearance you are likely to see her as both ugly and frightening. On the other hand, however outwardly ordinary your life, if you are open to becoming more than you are now, and you can see life, however blearily, with the eye of imagination, then the dakini is likely to manifest as beautiful, friendly, and enticing.

Some dakinis are part animal. They have the heads of boars, tigers, crows, bears, jackals, or a host of other strange creatures. Their bodies can be any of, or all of, the colours of the rainbow. Most usually, however, the dakini appears as a naked, dishevelled, witch-like woman, dancing in the sky of freedom that is her natural element.

In her naked and dishevelled dancing she also expresses total passionate involvement with the Dharma. She represents a state in which all your energies are aroused by it, in which you are prepared to give yourself shamelessly and totally to the search for Truth. For this reason, there are a number of yogic practices in which one visualizes oneself as a dakini, gazing upwards in devotion toward a Buddha, Bodhisattva, or great Buddhist teacher visualized in the sky above one's head. These practices are performed by both women and men, for we all need to open ourselves to a greater love and wisdom. In that sense, both men and women are feminine in relation to Enlightenment. To be filled with compassion and intuitive understanding you need to be devoted to them, to be completely receptive to their influence.

Buddhist Tantra recognizes different kinds of dakinis. In this chapter we shall focus mainly on dakinis whose appearances are direct expressions of the Enlightened mind, but we shall also briefly meet a few historical women teachers who are regarded as having that dakini quality.

## Vajrayogini and Vajravarahi

Let us look more closely at one of the most important of all dakinis. This is Vajrayogini (in Tibetan, Dorje Naljorma), whose name means something like 'the Dharma practitioner who embodies the diamond thunderbolt'. Like Tara, Vajrayogini usually appears as a sixteen-year-old girl, an age considered by Indians to be the prime of youth. She is a virgin, symbol of her complete innocence in relation to samsara. Her body is a brilliant, fascinating red – the colour of arousal and passion, for Vajrayogini is fiercely in love with the Dharma. She has flowing dishevelled black hair, for she has gone beyond concern for worldly appearances. She dances, abandoning herself to the inspiration of the Dharma.

In her right hand she brandishes a vajra-chopper above her head. This is a brutal implement, used by butchers for cutting and flaying. It has a vajra handle, and its blade is razor-sharp. With her chopper the dakini cuts off all attachment, especially concern for the physical body. For the faint-hearted, the brandished vajra-chopper is a threat of destruction. For the brave it is an invitation to approach and be cut free of all limitations. In her left hand she clasps to her heart the skull cup of shunyata, filled with the ambrosia of Great Bliss, for it is this supremely-satisfying nectar which the dakini pours out like wine to her devotees.

On her head is a tiara, for she is spiritually rich. However, rather than jewels, it is set with five human skulls. These are reminders of the wisdoms of the Five Buddhas in a form that cannot be ignored. Around her neck hangs a garland, not of flowers but of human skulls. There are usually fifty of them.

Over the hundreds of years for which Buddhist Tantra has been practised, symbolic attributes of these figures all gained layer upon layer of meaning. Some of these may seem to us quite technical, and rather distanced from the emotional power, even shock value, of the symbols themselves. These fifty heads that Vajrayogini wears are a good example of this. The Tantric tradition associates them (for technical reasons that I will not go into here) with the vowels and consonants of the Sanskrit alphabet and, by extension, with the idea that the dakini has purified speech on the subtlest level.

That explanation, while useful to certain Tantric practitioners, leads us a long way from the immediacy of those bleached skulls. The circle of heads suggests the endless round of birth and death. The dakini thrusts herself beyond it, and life and death become her ornaments. Thus she wears armlets, wristlets, and anklets of human bone. In the centre of her chest, secured by strings of bone, she sometimes wears a mirror in which all beings can see the effects of their past actions. These adornments are the dakini equivalents of silks and jewels – symbolizing the six perfections of the Bodhisattva.[31] While dakinis are beautiful and can appear in wondrous raiment, it is as though they are too close to the realities of existence to cover themselves in pretty, alluring things. They are Truth, and you can take them or leave them, they will not try to entice you. It is as though the Bodhisattvas such as Tara are the Dharma experienced in the warmth of the heart, and dakinis are the Dharma felt in one's guts.

In the crook of her left arm Vajrayogini holds a magic staff, similar to that of the great Tibetan guru Padmasambhava. This symbolizes her mystic male consort. Though she appears in female form, she is the perfect synthesis: feminine and masculine dancing together.

She dances with her right foot raised, so that her legs form a rough bow and arrow shape. The supporting left leg is the bow, the upraised right the arrow. The bow and arrow are important symbols in Tantra, symbolizing the inseparability of wisdom and its compassionate expression. With her left foot she is trampling on a prostrate human figure – symbol of the craving, hatred, and ignorance that she has subdued and which she now victoriously stamps into the ground. Yet she is not concerned with what is happening under her feet; her mastery of samsara is so total that she flattens obstacles effortlessly.

The whole movement of her being is upwards. Her hair stands on end. She leaps as she dances, as though impatient to take off into a higher dimension. In the centre of her forehead is a third eye, for she is able to see a higher truth, a wisdom beyond duality. All around her body flames leap upwards. They are the fires of her soaring inspiration, her unquenchable energy, her purifying wisdom. They are fires of love, burning for all that lives.

Her expression is ecstatic. She is drunk with wisdom, entranced with spiritual power, wild with compassion, insatiable for truth. At the same time her look is dangerous, warning. Like all dakinis, she does not fool around.

Vajrayogini appears in several forms other than her dancing one. For instance, she can have the same colours, implements, and so on, but be stepping to the left, with her right leg outstretched. In this form Vajrayogini is also sometimes called Sarvabuddhadakini (dakini of all the Buddhas), for she is that huge wave of passionate commitment to truth and total freedom that has carried all the Buddhas to Enlightenment. This time both her feet stamp on samsaric figures. In this position she no longer waves the chopper aloft. It is held loosely by her right side, as though it had done its work. Here she perhaps emphasizes the stage of the path beyond that at which you still need to cut down the promptings of samsara. If you have to cut them

SARVABUDDHADAKINI

down, you are still involved with them, still using energy in fighting them. Beyond this you reach a relaxed state, in which the mind can be left alone. Your understanding of reality is such that thoughts and emotions can be allowed to form themselves and dissolve away, like bubbles on a stream.

If her right hand has relaxed, her left now comes fully into play. The skull cup is no longer held to her heart but aloft, to her lips. Her head is tilted back as she pours into her mouth a steady flow of the red light-nectar of Great Bliss, which looks just like blood. Blood is life, and the dakini drinks incessantly, becoming filled with spiritual zest and energy. It is also sometimes said she is drinking the blood of the Maras – all the hindering forces that prevent one from finding Enlightened freedom. Her large breasts are thrust forward, symbolizing her capacity to bestow Great Bliss on all beings.

Another form of this dakini who is almost identical to the dancing form is Vajravarahi (Tibetan: Dorje Phamo).[32] Vajravarahi means 'diamond sow'. This refers to the one characteristic that distinguishes her from Vajrayogini – the head of a sow that appears in her piled-up hair. The pig or sow is a Buddhist symbol for ignorance. It appears at the centre of the Wheel of Life (a graphic description of how we trap ourselves in the cycle of suffering) in a kind of dance with the snake of hatred and the cock of craving. The three career round in a circle, each biting the tail of the one in front. The sow in Vajravarahi's hair is like a trophy. She has severed the head of the sow of ignorance with her vajra-chopper, and brought the drunken dance of suffering to an end.

Vajrayogini or Vajravarahi play a very important role in the highest level of Buddhist Tantra, both alone and in connection with the male figure known as Heruka.[33] Heruka is usually blue in colour, and frequently represented as a standing figure with twelve arms. He and Vajrayogini are in passionate sexual embrace. Her left hand, holding a skull cup, is around his neck. Her right, holding a vajra or a vajra-chopper, is raised. The fingers of her right hand are making a gesture of driving away negative forces.

The visualization of Heruka and Vajrayogini in sexual embrace is particularly recommended for those of passionate temperament, who tend to craving rather than aversion. The meditation sublimates craving and refines sexual energy. On the highest level the two figures symbolize the union of wisdom (symbolized by Vajrayogini) and compassion (Heruka). Also, through deep inner concentration in Tantric meditation one can develop intensely blissful states of mind, and then use these to explore the nature of reality. So Heruka and Vajrayogini also embody Enlightened states of consciousness in which Great Bliss is suffused with the understanding of emptiness.

*You are the Vajrayogini!*
*Holding back has ended.*
*You have taken the great dive into life*
*By dying in the flames of Shunyata.*
*And you have won the Great Bliss*
*By giving up and losing*
*Your sense of separateness.*

*All care has been thrown aside*
*All caution gone,*
*And you remain,*
*Proud great dancer on your sun throne,*
*Laughing a laugh*
*That knows no sorrow.*
*You have forgotten everything*
*So you wear your ornaments of bone*
*And your garland of heads.*[34]

## Kurukulla and the Rite of Fascination

The function of our next dakini, Kurukulla, is to fascinate. Like Vajrayogini, she is brilliant red, naked except for bone ornaments, and dancing. However, rather than a vajra-chopper and a skull cup, she holds a flowery bow and arrow. Sometimes she has four arms, and as well as the bow and arrow she holds a hook and a noose. These implements, as well as the red colour of her body, are associated with the Tantric function of fascination. Buddhist Tantra took over magical rites that were being used in India at the time and redirected them. Naturally, there were many forms of love magic in ancient India, through which a woman or man would try to cause someone to fall hopelessly in love with them. These rituals of love magic were refashioned by the Buddhist Tantric practitioners so that they could be used to cause someone to fall hopelessly in love with the Dharma, with wisdom and compassion.

When looking at Red Tara, to whom Kurukulla is related, we saw that the bow and arrow made of flowers are the weapons of Kamadeva, the Indian god of love. By a kind of love-magic Kurukulla leads even enemies of the Dharma to fall at her feet. Having shot her victims, she pulls them in with the hook and binds them with the noose. Some of her Tantric rituals are not for the squeamish, and perhaps come a little close to black magic. After all, Buddhism is all about freedom. Using magical means to coerce someone to follow the path to freedom against their will is rather contradictory.

Perhaps the most extraordinary of all these red dakini forms is one described in the *Sadhanamala*, and associated with the tradition of Savaripa. Here she is standing in an aggressive stance, holding the vajra-chopper in her right hand and her own head – which she has severed – in her left. She is flanked by the dakinis Vajravairocani and Vajravarnani. Three streams of blood spurt

KURUKULLA

from the headless neck and flow into her own mouth and the mouths of the two dakinis. The severing of the head symbolizes the cutting off of all ego-discrimination.

We have seen that not all dakinis are emanations of emptiness. There are a number of great female Tantric teachers who achieved the 'status' of dakinis and are often represented in dancing dakini form. We have already met Niguma. She was the disciple and Tantric consort of the Indian teacher Naropa, who is known particularly for the very important set of six Tantric yogas named after him. Niguma became a great teacher in her own right, and started an important parallel lineage of the 'six yogas'. So now we shall turn to a couple of human beings who are considered to be dakinis, and are frequently represented in dakini form in Tibetan paintings.

## Machik Labdron: Letting Go of the Body

Machik Labdron (1055–1153) was a Tibetan woman who, in her youth, supported herself by reading the Perfection of Wisdom volumes. Patrons would employ her to read the texts aloud to gain merit, and she excelled at reading. (Not, as we might imagine in the West, because of the clarity and beauty with which she read, but because of her speed!) Reading these scriptures, she herself began to gain insight into the Perfection of Wisdom. Later she met an Indian teacher called Phadampa Sangye who taught her a form of the extraordinary meditation known as the Chöd rite.

The Chöd is a dramatized enactment of the principles of the Dharma. It is also a very powerful test of your 'spiritual nerve'. To do it you go to an isolated, awe-inspiring place, such as a cremation ground. Then, after various preliminaries, you see your consciousness separate from your body and become a dakini. The dakini then chops what is now your corpse to pieces and places them in a gigantic skull cauldron. Through the use of mantra, the pieces of the corpse are all transmuted into a wondrous nectar, which is then increased and multiplied so that it becomes vast. This ocean of nectar is then offered to all Enlightened beings out of devotion, and to all mundane beings out of compassion. Included among the mundane beings are all the local ghosts and spirits of the isolated place in which you are performing the rite, as well as all who may wish you harm.

So the Chöd rite is a particularly effective way of making real to yourself Dharma teachings that might otherwise remain on the level of ideas. You come face to face with your own death – both of the body and the ego. You invoke everything that is fearful and terrifying, and have to call on a state of complete confidence in the Dharma, beyond hope and fear, in order to withstand it. You also have to practise tremendous generosity, giving away the physical body, which is our most prized possession, for the benefit of all living beings. Out of her deep understanding, derived from many years of practice, Machik developed a new form of the Chöd Rite, which has since been incorporated into all schools of Tibetan Buddhism. Machik Labdron is herself commonly shown as a white dancing dakini. As she dances she plays a double-sided drum with her right hand, and rings a vajra-bell with her left.

## Yeshe Tsogyal: Hidden Teachings

Another famous and highly-attained Tibetan woman is Yeshe Tsogyal, who lived in the eighth century and was one of the main disciples, and a Tantric consort, of the great Indian guru Padmasambhava, who played a crucial part in establishing Buddhism in Tibet. She practised his teachings, specializing particularly in meditation on a Tantric deity called Vajrakila –

'diamond dagger'. Eventually she came to the highest realization. After Padmasambhava left Tibet, Yeshe Tsogyal became an important teacher in her own right. She was also responsible for writing down and concealing many of the *termas* left by Padmasambhava. These we could call Dharma time-capsules – teachings that have been hidden in out-of-the-way places until they are needed. Padmasambhava is credited with the clairvoyant ability to see into future ages and teach the Dharma in forms suitable for the particular needs of those times. It is those teachings which Yeshe Tsogyal disseminated through Tibet. According to some sources, Yeshe Tsogyal was Vajravarahi in human form, and also an incarnation of Tara and Locana. She is often shown in dakini form, with skull cup and vajra-chopper.

## The Lion-Headed Dakini

Lastly we come to a figure who, according to the Nyingma school, is Padmasambhava himself appearing as a dakini (which ought to dispel any fixed ideas we have of 'spiritual appearances' corresponding to physical gender). He appears as the Lion-Faced or Lion-Headed One (Sanskrit: Simhamukha or Simhavaktra). She is a particularly powerful guardian dakini, invoked in the exorcism of hindering forces. She is dark blue in colour, dancing with vajra-chopper and skull cup. Her head is that of a lion. Sometimes she is depicted flanked by two other dakinis with animal heads: one a tiger, the other a bear.

## The Dakini Within

So far I have mainly spoken of dakinis as though they were externally existent beings, to be found in ancient Indian cremation grounds and the wildernesses of Tibet. But where is the real wilderness, the true cremation ground, to be found? Tilopa, in teaching Naropa, repeatedly tells him:

*Look into the mirror of your mind*
*The mysterious home of the dakini.*

To understand how we can meet dakinis within our own mind, we need to look more closely at what the dakinis symbolize. In essence, dakinis are all those experiences, both internal and external, that inspire us and spur us on to practise the Dharma. Internally, the dakini is all those outpourings of something higher and more spontaneous within us that make us feel we are on the right track, that we are making progress on the spiritual path. This does not mean they are simply comforting. Occasionally they may be shattering, like lightning flashes of insight that turn our view of ourselves and the world completely upside down.

Whether we find the dakinis' presence enjoyable or terrifying depends on our degree of openness to them. If we meet them wholeheartedly, they come to us as feelings of inspiration, moods of great happiness and exhilaration, dauntless courage, sudden laughter, or total relaxation, the urge to give of ourselves completely, bursts of energy, poetry, and song. All these experiences on the highest level are gifts of the dakinis. The dakinis, you could say, are the muses of the transcendental.

Like the muses, the dakinis are not controllable. They burst forth from higher levels of the mind (their 'mysterious home'). All we can do is create the right conditions for them to appear. We invite the dakini, and await developments. We do this mainly by Going for Refuge to the Three Jewels: the Buddha, Dharma, and Sangha; by committing ourselves wholeheartedly to the path; and by doing our best to carry that commitment through.

However, I ought not to talk too blithely about inviting dakinis. A word of warning: do not invite them unless you mean it. If you prove to be a fraud, or not to have the courage of your convictions – if you ostensibly commit yourself but then avoid the consequences – the dakinis may leave you in disgust. (If we look at our lives we find that inspiration often disappears after we have ducked a challenge.) They may even threaten you – or that is how it may feel. If you are on the run from the truth, on the run from your own creative energies, you will feel as though they are turning against you. You can end up feeling like a lion-tamer whose courage has drained away, watching the lionesses beginning to jump off their stools and close in on you.

Dakinis do not stand on ceremony. Nor do they care about convention. They understand that all forms are emptiness. Dakinis are the unexpected, the spontaneous. They are the opposite of the safe security of one's ego prison. A dakini may search for years (like Leonora for Floristan in Beethoven's *Fidelio*) seeking an opportunity to rescue you from the dungeon of craving and ignorance. When she suddenly appears in the darkness to cut you free from your shackles, you had better want to go with her.

To follow her is a risk. If you do you will never be quite the same again. Dakinis are wrathful and passionate. They always spell death for the ego. If you are ready, if you delight in her appearance and rejoice in her unpredictability, you will find she gives death and birth. In exchange for suffering the blow of her vajra-chopper you will experience a new and unimaginable freedom. She will then allow you to enter her dance, to dance into the fire, the flames of spiralling inspiration and ecstatic creativity. She will bestow her gifts on you: wisdom, Great Bliss, the experience of non-duality, total liberation.

To start with, however, even though we may be committed and making an effort to practise the Dharma, the dakini is likely to be elusive. For a while she appears in a certain spiritual practice, a certain Dharma teaching, a certain person even, and we feel enriched and inspired. Then she moves, shifts, changes shape. She changes her forms more often than a fashion-conscious woman changes her wardrobe. If you are attached to the forms she takes on, the clothes she might wear, you will be left treasuring only a scarf or a shawl as a souvenir. The third of the ten fetters to Enlightenment enumerated by the Buddha was 'attachment to rites and rituals as ends in themselves'. This does not mean that ritual has no place in Buddhism. The Buddha just denies that there is any point in going through the motions of any spiritual practice as an end in itself.

It is easy to become chained to particular aspects of spiritual practice. The wonderful meditation experience you once had can become a trophy, a party piece to trot out to impress your friends. A piece of Buddhist teaching which you have found helpful may become your dogmatic prescription for everyone. The dakini, though, is reborn in every moment. She is in no particular form of practice or teaching. We have to strive to see her as she is in herself – the naked, voluptuous Truth. Once we have met her face to face in that way, she will appear to us in all forms. We shall recognize her unerringly in all aspects of existence, hear her crooning her song of the Dharma everywhere, for she is our own purified consciousness. To elaborate on Tilopa's advice, once our mind is a mirror, cleansed and spotless, then we shall see that it is 'the home of the dakini'.

To arrive at this stage requires a great letting-go. The dakini's halo of flames and her total nakedness point to the burning off, the stripping away, of everything inessential. Higher states of consciousness are characterized by their total simplicity. To become one with the dakini we have to follow the counsel of Padmasambhava, the great Indian teacher, whose contribution was crucial in establishing Buddhism in Tibet:

*Let these three expressions: I do not have, I do not understand, I*
*do not know, be repeated over and over again. That is the heart*
*of my advice.*[35]

Once this is achieved, you will be the dakini, the true free dancer
in the limitless sky of Liberation.

## The Dakini Outside

I have said that the dakini represents those inspiring forces
which carry you along the path. Through visualizing a dakini in
meditation, you call up those energies within yourself. The difference between having to rely purely on your everyday energy
to follow the path and being in touch with the dakini within is
like the difference between trudging across muddy terrain and
hang-gliding over it. Hang-gliding is fast, free, exhilarating, and
spiced with a certain risk. Conversely, without at least occasional
flashes of inspiration you can tire of the effort involved in painfully picking a path between the potholes. Thankfully, when
your inner dakinis refuse to come out to play (for dakinis are
playful – if they have gone away perhaps you have been too
tense in your approach) there is still the possibility of deriving
inspiration from an external dakini – from another human being
who has dakini qualities.

This can be understood on a number of different levels. At the
highest level, we could have the good fortune to meet with a
highly realized woman who can teach us the Dharma. As someone who has come to embody the dakini principle, she can help
us to free ourselves from suffering and limitation, and to enter
the blue sky of freedom through directly realizing the emptiness
of inherent existence of all phenomena – including what we
think of as 'me'.

Secondly, advanced practitioners of the Buddhist Tantric yogas may, at a certain stage of their development, be encouraged to engage in sexual yoga with a qualified partner. This yoga enables them to focus their energies very strongly, to concentrate deep within themselves. The enhanced power of concentration produced by this sexual yoga enables them to deepen their realization of emptiness. For a man, the more his partner has the dakini qualities, the more effective this practice is likely to be. (The same applies in the reverse case, where a woman will be helped if her partner has as much as possible of the qualities of a daka.)

Naturally enough, people are often very curious about these sexual yogas, but they belong to a very advanced stage of Buddhist practice indeed. One can do oneself far more harm than good by fantasizing about practising them, let alone actually doing so, before one is ready. Unfortunately there will always be men who like the idea of dressing up their sexual encounters as Tantric practice, and women who fancy the idea of themselves as spiritual consorts. But if you really want to dance in the sky, first you have to learn to keep your feet on the ground.

As it is a pretty safe assumption that we are not highly advanced Tantric adepts, can we find a dakini outside? I think there is a way in which we can helpfully think of doing so, though it is widening the traditional definition of the dakini a little. We can approach it if we think of the three central values of Buddhism. These are known as the Three Jewels or Three Refuges: the Buddha, the ideal of Enlightenment; the Dharma, his teaching of the path; and the Sangha, the community of realized Buddhist practitioners. In Tantric Buddhism these central values are expressed in an additional way, in what are known as the Three Roots, or the Three Esoteric Refuges. These are the guru, the teacher who points out to you the way to Enlightenment; the yidam, the Tantric deity on whom you meditate; and the dakini.

These Three Roots, we could say, are the Three Jewels within our own experience. For example, we may never have met a Buddha, but the person who comes closest to him in our own life experience is our spiritual teacher. So these Three Roots are 'esoteric' in the sense that they are matters of direct experience.

The dakini is the esoteric Sangha Refuge. The purpose of the sangha in general is to inspire and encourage us on the path to freedom. But although we may find the sangha in general inspiring, for the Tantra this is not enough. The Esoteric Refuges are personal. We could even call them the 'intimate' Refuges. They are the aspects of the Esoteric Refuges with which we feel a direct link, and to which we have made an individual commitment. Though Sangha members may be encouraging and helpful, that does not qualify them to be our dakini Refuge. However, if there is a fellow Dharma practitioner with whom we have direct personal communication, and whose company and example stir up our energy to practise the Dharma, that person could be said to act for us as a kind of dakini or daka. They may be a woman or a man, sixteen years old or eighty, no matter. The criterion is that in their presence we call up more energy for our efforts to follow the path. They wake us up. They get us moving.

If we find such a person it is no good sitting around hoping they will be our friend. We just have to commit ourselves to being a friend to *them*. If we are active, giving to them and helping them, then if they have that dakini or daka quality they will respond.

Once again, as with the inner dakini, we had better mean it. Spiritual friendship is demanding. It is fuelled by authentic communication. It is close; there are strong feelings involved. Nonetheless, there can hardly be anything so deeply satisfying, and so pleasurable, as a spiritual friendship with someone who for us has that dakini quality.

In such a friendship two people work to take down the barriers between them. They let go of thinking of their own needs, of fear of self-revelation and intimacy. They try to let go of everything and give themselves to the Dharma, to a mutual exploration of the Truth. They take delight in that Truth, knowing that they are together in this evanescent form so briefly that their meeting has never been before and will never be again, and that in the moment they are both unknowable. When two separate individuals are united in the Dharma, there we find the play, the true dance, of the dakinis.

# 6

## FEMALE PROTECTORS

### Introduction:
### The Hideous Damsel and the Tantric Protectress

In one of the stories of King Arthur and his Knights of the Round Table, we find the knight Parsifal on the Grail Quest. Born in a humble place, with a name that means 'innocent fool', he is yet one of the greatest of all knights. Early in his career he finds his way to the Grail Castle, but fails to ask a crucial question, and soon finds himself alone. As a pure and accomplished knight, he succeeds in defeating many opponents and sending them back to Arthur's court. As a result he becomes famous, and Arthur and his knights go to seek him out. Once they have found him they hold a great feast in his honour. For three days they praise and honour Parsifal. It is when the feast is at its height, and Parsifal has been praised to the skies, that a woman turns up, uninvited.

She is an ugly old crone, mounted on a decrepit old mule. Her eyes are like those of a rat, her nose like that of a cat or a monkey, her lips would better suit an ass or a bull than a human being. She has facial hair, a humped back, and her hips and shoulders are gnarled and twisted like tree roots. She has black braided hair, and hands and nails that are 'iron dark'. Naturally enough, her appearance (in both senses of the word) spoils the celebration. She then completely ruins things for Parsifal by reciting a long list of all his faults and failings, culminating in his failure to ask the crucial question in the Grail Castle. Parsifal is humiliated in front of all those who had been toasting his greatness and achievements.

The Old Crone, or Hideous Damsel as she is often called, is a powerful archetypal figure. For both women and men she represents the ruin of all mundane success, the humbling of all confidence based on worldly attributes and achievements. For women and men who base their self-worth on their physical attractiveness, she is old age, wrinkles, grey hairs, and fatty tissue. For men and women ambitious to succeed and make their mark on the world, she is the empty feeling that comes upon them in middle age, after they have achieved all that they dreamed of: a sense of 'so what?' and 'is that all?'

Nobody wants the Hideous Damsel to turn up. When we are preening ourselves in the mirror and we see the silhouette of that old mule limp into view in the distance, bearing its hunched burden, the natural tendency is to turn and run. However, she is one of the best friends that a man or woman could have, for it is dangerous for us to rest on our egotistical laurels, enjoying our looks, our wealth, or our status, basking in a self-satisfied sense of having made it – whatever 'it' may be for us. It makes us lazy and selfish, and it lulls us into a false sense of security. For the fact is that mundane life always ends in tears. At death, if not much sooner, we shall lose all our everyday sources of comfort and self-worth.

So it is a gift for us when the Hideous Damsel turns up unannounced – the hooves of her old mule leaving filthy marks on our best carpet – and breaks the spell of our self-satisfaction. She brings us down to earth, reminding us that the true achievement of our life is to make something of ourselves spiritually. By reciting the litany of our faults and failings she shows us how much inner work we still have to do. When we have settled for external success, she points us once more in the direction of the Grail of spiritual fulfilment.

Women may identify with the Hideous Damsel for negative and positive reasons. Unable to cope with life's demands, some may just give up on life and on themselves and 'let themselves go'. They no longer make any effort with their appearance, no longer bother if the house is tidy, if their work is up to standard, or their children are dressed properly for school. The bag lady has often been swallowed by the negative side of the Hideous Damsel. From a positive perspective a woman may go deeply into the Dharma and come to a point where she lets go of all concerns about how people view her. She gives up bothering with the usual social games, and simply becomes terrifyingly herself.

A man may find that after much adventuring, charging around on noble steeds (or in Ford Mustangs) he has made a name for himself, but it all means nothing to him. Perhaps he may even have been practising Buddhism for many years, and found that his initial great enthusiasm for the quest for Enlightenment has worn off. At this point he is well advised to leave behind his swift horse with its fancy saddle and hitch a ride on that limping old mule. The pace may seem painfully slow, but at least he has time to take in the details of the terrain through which he is passing, and he can be sure he is being taken in the right direction.

The main task of the Hideous Damsel is to save us from ourselves, to protect us from our own pride, arrogance, and self-satisfaction. These cause us great suffering, as they cut us off from others and the world around us. It is not surprising, therefore, that the Hideous Damsel should turn up in a number of forms in Buddhist Tantra as a protector figure. Some of these Dharma protectors are visualized in extremely frightening and seemingly dangerous forms. Often they are indigenous Indian or Tibetan deities who have been converted to the Dharma by some great Tantric yogi or yogini, and have vowed to help those who practise it.

If we relate to these protectors as external forces, then they serve two functions. They protect Buddhist practitioners and Buddhist teachings, warding off external threats. They also ensure that those who have embarked on the Tantric path do not misuse their powers or backslide. Internally, they represent the powerful energies that are unleashed in an advanced Dharma practitioner, which come to their aid when they are faced with difficulties and obstacles. These figures are not to be treated lightly or without respect, and their practices are best left to those meditators who are well qualified to handle the energies they embody. Yet knowing about them, as with all these figures, tells us something about our own minds, about our potential as human beings.

There are many female protector figures in the Buddhist Tantra. In this chapter we shall focus on two that stem from Indian tradition, and later became of great importance to Tibetan Buddhism. Here comes the first one, riding a mule....

## Shridevi: the Glorious Goddess

Shridevi, the 'glorious goddess' (Tibetan: Paldan Lhamo), takes various forms, but she usually has a wrathful appearance: dark blue, ferocious, with three bloodshot eyes. Her red flaming hair stands on end, and above her head is a fan of peacock feathers. She has sharp fangs, and laughs with a sound like thunder. She is riding on a mule which is galloping furiously over a sea of blood.

SHRIDEVI

It is said that she is riding towards Siberia, after an unsuccessful attempt to convert the king of (Sri) Lanka to Buddhism. Her mule has been hit by the vengeful king's arrow. The wound in its flank has been transformed into a wisdom eye.

She is almost naked, and her body is wreathed in snakes and adorned with bone ornaments and a necklace of skulls. In her left hand she bears a brimming skull cup. In her right she holds aloft a black skull-topped staff. Flames roar and black storm-clouds swirl around her as she gallops along. From her saddle hangs a pouch with dice. (Her initiation is held to be a gateway to divinatory powers, and she can be invoked by practitioners of *mo*, the Tibetan system of divination, which often involves the use of dice.) She sits side-saddle on the flayed skin of her own son.

According to one tradition, Shridevi was given various gifts by other deities. She received the dice from the Tantric deity Hevajra in order to determine the life of men. She received the fan of peacock feathers from Brahma (one of the most important Hindu gods, who was incorporated into Tantric Buddhism as a minor protector). Vajrapani, the Bodhisattva associated with spiritual power and energy, gave her a hammer, and various other deities gave her a lion and a serpent, which she wears as earrings, and her mule, which has deadly snakes for reins.

Shridevi brandishes her staff to threaten all obstacles to the success of the Dharma. Her terrible form serves as a warning to Tantric practitioners of the fearsome states into which they may fall if they fail to keep the pledges taken at the time of initiation. Tantric practitioners acknowledge that the meditations they practise enable them to accumulate a great deal of psychic power. A person who engages in advanced Tantric practice but no longer feels bound to use the power he or she has gained for ethical purposes is thus a great danger to themselves and others. Someone who uses the energy and accomplishments derived from a Tantric sadhana to gratify their own ego rather than laying it at the service of all sentient beings is basically engaging in black magic. Figures like Shridevi have the power to subdue those who abuse their power and render them harmless. She protects those who practise the Dharma from hindrances and enemies, and she guards the Dharma itself from being misused – when of course it ceases to become the Dharma.

Not only can Shridevi control dark external forces; she is capable of pacifying all those hindering inner forces that bind us to the 'wheel of fire' of mundane existence. Hence she is also known in Tibet as 'the one who overpowers and crushes the hosts of the passions' (Paldan Makzor Gyalmo). The tradition that she is seated on the skin of her own son suggests perhaps her complete overcoming of all attachment, for of all emotional connections that between mother and child is probably the strongest.

Shridevi is the female companion of the male protector Mahakala: 'the great black one'. He is a wrathful emanation of the peaceful and compassionate Avalokita. Like Mahakala, the powerful and terrifying Shridevi also has a gentle form. Her peaceful manifestation is known as Ekamatri Shridevi (Tibetan: Machik Paldan Lhamo). Dressed in celestial clothing, she sits on a lotus in the posture of royal ease, her left foot slightly extended. She wears a Bodhisattva crown of jewels, and smiles compassionately. In her left hand she holds a bowl filled with jewels. In her right is a standard with pennants in all the colours of the rainbow. Her body is surrounded by an aura of brilliant light.

In fact there are many forms of Shridevi, and different schools of Tibetan Buddhism may regard one or another of them as their special protector.[36] In the fifteenth century she was 'appointed' Dharma protectress of Ganden, one of the great Tibetan monasteries, by the first Dalai Lama. Ever since then she has been a special protectress of the Dalai Lamas. The fifth Dalai Lama wrote instructions for meditating upon her, and a scroll painting of Shridevi travels with the Dalai Lamas wherever they go. For centuries this picture was kept unseen in its red case. But in 1940 the present Dalai Lama, then aged about seven and on his way to be enthroned, was met close to Lhasa by a great crowd of officials and notables, including his three main servants, one of whom had brought the painting, hidden as usual in its case. On seeing it near the entrance to his tent, he promptly grabbed it, took it inside, and opened it. The picture that had not been unveiled for so long was revealed. The Dalai Lama surveyed it and then replaced it in its case. Everyone present was amazed at what he had done.

Shridevi has a retinue. It is so large that that a description of it would fill a whole iconographical book. It includes the four Queens of the Seasons, the five Goddesses of Long Life, and twelve goddesses known as *tanrungmas*. These are indigenous Tibetan deities who have been converted to the Dharma and now guard and protect the practitioners of various meditation lineages.

Shridevi also has in her retinue a type of female protectress known as *mahakali*. They are generally mounted on horses or mules, with goatskin bags of poison hanging from their saddles. They have bows and arrows, and lassos made of snakes. They each wear a mirror, in which all one's karma is reflected. They are swift-acting and ferocious against enemies of the Dharma.

> *Bhyoh!*
> *Mind-essence working the four miraculous activities,*
> *Not deviant from the essence, neither being mind alone,*
> *Absolute indivisible, free of color or form,*
> *Her miracles mere magic, fitting each being's mind;*
> *She manifests, she the ferocious Glory Goddess!*
>
> *Fierce-maker, Fierce Being, her reality is ferocious,*
> *Chief Lady of the retinue of the fierce,*
> *Her symbolic body a glistening dark black!*
> *I bow to the all-terrifying Mother Goddess!*
> *Fiercely pray free of diseases, demons, foes, and obstructions![37]*

## Ekajata: Guardian of the Teachings

The Nyingma school is the oldest form of Buddhism in Tibet and calls on many protectors rarely or never invoked by other schools. These Nyingma protectors appear in some of the most horrific forms imaginable. They are such stuff as nightmares and psychotic hallucinations are made on. They are your worst fears, the creatures you knew were lurking in the darkness when as a child you hid under the bedclothes but could not sleep. Nonetheless, while commanding a healthy respect from their devotees, these strange figures call forth reverence and devotion in the Tantric practitioner, just as much as do the benignly-smiling Buddhas.

Of particular importance for the Nyingma school is a set of three protectors: the male Rahula and Dorje Lekpa, and the no less formidable Ekajata (or Ekajati), which means 'the goddess with a single plait of hair'.[38] Singularity, or the uncompromising vision of things from the highest viewpoint, seems to be the message of this figure. She is dark and menacing, surrounded by flames, and nearly naked. Her skull-crowned hair writhes upwards. Her face contorts with fury. Her brows are knitted and she has only one eye, in the middle of her forehead. From her ugly mouth a single fang protrudes. She is often depicted with only one breast. She is wreathed in severed heads. With her right hand she waves a stake on which is impaled a living human figure. In her left hand she displays the heart of a foe of the Dharma that she has ripped out.

Ekajata is the supreme protectress of the Dzogchen teachings, the highest and most precious of all Nyingma practices. She also functions as a guardian of mantras – preventing them from being disclosed to those unworthy to use them, and ensuring that those who have been empowered to use them do so for appropriate purposes. She may perhaps guard them in a more general sense as well, preventing them from losing their power and efficacy, or from being lost altogether.

Like Shridevi, Ekajata can assume a number of different forms and colours. Characteristically she is dark brown, though she can also be red or blue. In different forms she can hold various implements or weapons. For instance, one scholar describes forms holding a trident, a heart, and a snare; a trident and skull cup; the heart of an enemy and a 'clever falcon'.[39] She can also, on occasion, dispatch numerous female wolves as messengers.

Ekajata also appears, in a slightly less terrifying form, as an attendant on Green Tara, along with red Marici, the goddess of the dawn. In this context she has two eyes and so forth, and holds a vajra-chopper and a skull cup, and is described as sky blue, wrathful, but loving and bright. By an extension of this role, she came to be seen as a kind of blue form of Tara, known as Ugra Tara, or Tara the Ferocious.

*Mistress of the sacred lands and places,*
*Manifestation Ekajati,*
*Chief of the myriad demonesses,*
*Powerful queen of the three worlds,*
*Protectress of the Great Secret Teachings,*
*Great guardian of the Highest Teaching,*
*Dark-brown queen,*
*One-eyed vajra mother,*
*Your ferocious round eye*
*Clearly beholds the three realms of existence.*[40]

As we have seen, Buddhist Tantra is interested in integrating all expressions of energy into the path to Enlightenment. Here we see it engaging with energy expressing itself though the archetype of the old crone, or old witch. Even when life gets ugly, when it seems set on devouring us, still for the Tantric practitioner such circumstances can be incorporated into the path.

# 7

## KUAN-YIN: HEARING THE CRIES OF THE WORLD

### From India to China: Compassion Changes Gender

So far, all the figures we have met have come from the Indo-Tibetan tradition. It is now time to travel further east to encounter a female Bodhisattva who has played a very important role in Buddhism in Japan, Korea, and above all in China. What is extraordinary about this figure is that this Bodhisattva was originally depicted as male.

We have already met the male Bodhisattva Avalokita, the embodiment of infinite tenderness and compassion for all living beings. We have seen too how that compassion came to be embodied also in female form, as Tara is said to have been born from Avalokita's tears. Thus in Tibet, which inherited much of Indian Tantric Buddhism, both the male Avalokita (of whom the Dalai Lama is said to be an emanation) and Tara were venerated and meditated upon. However, in China the cult of Tara never gained any great importance. Instead, as the centuries went by, the figure of Avalokita, known in China as Kuan Yin, (or

Guanyin, depending how you transliterate it) underwent a
change from male to female.

Texts relating to Avalokita were translated into Chinese as
early as the third century CE. Within a couple of hundred years
he had become quite a well-known figure in Chinese Buddhism,
and by the eighth century he was very popular indeed. At this
point a Tantric sutra was translated into Chinese which described a female form of the Bodhisattva, dressed in white. From
the tenth century onwards, paintings of this form began to appear. This form was known in China as Pai-i Kuan Yin, which literally means 'the white-clad Kuan Yin'. Over the succeeding
centuries Kuan Yin gained millions of devotees, and acquired
many different forms. It is really only with the Communist takeover in China that Kuan Yin has been forced, apparently at least,
to flee the country. Devotion to her continues in the non-Com-
munist Chinese-speaking world, as well as in Japan, where she is
known as Kwannon.

The academic jury is still out on the question of how and why
Kuan Yin changed gender in China. If we look at the development of Indian Buddhism, and its flowering in Tibet and China,
we can see common themes, but the figures develop in different
ways. The source, symbolically at least, of all these later developments is Amitabha, the Buddha of Infinite Light, often depicted
as ruby-red in colour, who is symbolically connected with the
West and the setting sun. In Tantric Buddhism, he is the head of
the Lotus family, which is especially associated with the qualities
of love and compassion. Avalokita is said to have appeared from
a ray of light emanated by Amitabha.

We saw in the chapter on the female consorts of the Five
Buddhas that Amitabha's discriminating wisdom is embodied in
the figure of Pandaravasini, whose name means 'the
white-robed', so it may be no coincidence that the earliest form
of female Kuan Yin in China was the white-clad Kuan Yin. It

could well be that some of Pandaravasini's qualities, or perhaps those of White Tara, or both, became incorporated into the figure of Avalokiteshvara, causing his change of gender.

It seems too that all the main qualities of Enlightenment can be embodied in either male or female forms – just as they can be developed by actual men and women. So as Buddhism developed, wisdom came to be particularly embodied in the forms of both the Wisdom Goddess and Manjushri. Similarly, compassion could not remain a male prerogative, as it were. In yab-yum forms, it was the female figures who especially embodied wisdom and the male figures compassion or skilful means. So with Avalokiteshvara as the most important Bodhisattva of compassion, the psychic situation called for the appearance of a female equivalent. In Indo-Tibetan Buddhism this need was fulfilled by the many forms of Tara, whereas Chinese Buddhism went down another route, and transformed Avalokiteshvara into the female forms of Kuan Yin.

This development is even more understandable, as a mother's love for her child is a very powerful metaphor for the universal compassion for all beings felt by the advanced Bodhisattva. This is not to say that women are necessarily better at developing universal compassion than men. But it is frequently the case that our strongest experience of unconditional love comes from our mother, and we often draw on that, consciously or unconsciously, when we start trying to develop love and compassion for all beings.

## The Move from Sight to Sound

Not only did Avalokita undergo a sex-change in China; his name also subtly changed meaning. Avalokita's full name is Avalokiteshvara, which means 'the Lord who sees' or, as it is sometimes

KUAN YIN

translated, 'the Lord who looks down'. Eyes are an important
feature of the symbolism of the Lotus family. Avalokiteshvara is
sometimes said to have been born from a ray of light emanating
from Amitabha's right eye. As we have seen, the tears from
Avalokiteshvara's eyes gave birth to Tara. The white form of Tara
has seven wisdom eyes. Amitabha's symbolic animal is the peacock, whose beautiful tail feathers are each marked with a pat-
tern reminiscent of an eye. All this probably relates to the
discriminating wisdom of Amitabha, which can discern the
unique features of every experience. Thus Avalokiteshvara is often represented as surveying the world, looking down upon it.
Sometimes, as in the *Heart Sutra*, when he looks down at the
world he penetrates its true, insubstantial nature, but more often he focuses upon the endless ocean of suffering on which

living beings are tossed. In response, compassion pours from his heart in the form of his famous mantra: *om mani padme hum*.

With so much emphasis on sight, it is interesting that the name Avalokiteshvara was translated into Chinese as Kuan Yin, for this name means 'the one who hears sounds'. Sometimes it is rendered as Kuan Shih Yin – 'the one who hears the sounds of the world'. These sounds are presumably the cries of suffering and desire for freedom that are uttered by living beings, and Kuan Yin does not just hear them: she listens to every cry, takes it to heart, and responds. As with Avalokiteshvara's change of gender, it is not entirely clear why his name was translated in this way. Admittedly, it would take only a slight misspelling of his name for it to mean 'the one who hears sounds'. But several Chinese translators rendered it in the same way, which makes it unlikely to be a mistake.

This Chinese association of Avalokiteshvara, and therefore of Kuan Yin, with hearing may be connected with a Buddhist text called in Sanskrit the *Samadhi Sutra*. (Its Chinese name means 'The Buddha's Great Crown Sutra'.) In this sutra, Manjushri, the Bodhisattva of wisdom, is asked by the Buddha to evaluate twenty-five methods of meditation to see which is best suited to the needs of his disciple Ananda, and to those of disciples in future times. Each method is described and praised by a different advanced disciple of the Buddha. When his turn comes, Avalokiteshvara describes a method of meditating on sound. Manjushri chooses this as the most effective meditation method. What is interesting about this sutra is that although it has a Sanskrit title, it is now generally accepted by scholars to have been written in China and passed off as a translation of an Indian Buddhist text. So it seems that, for whatever reason, there was more than one aspect to the attempt to associate Avalokiteshvara with hearing rather than sight in China.

## Forms of Kuan Yin

As I write this I have on my desk a small metal statue of Kuan Yin given me by a friend. The figure stands on a lotus flower, around which lap ocean waves. She is dressed in a long flowing gown, whose many folds give life and grace to the figure. The gown culminates in a hood, which covers her head. She is adorned with a necklace of jewels. Her right hand is raised in a gesture of blessing, while her left is held open at the level of her navel. Standing up in her left palm is a long, slender vase, which contains the nectar of immortality. She has a mature, rounded face, with a serene expression. The overall impression of the statue is stately, dignified, and peaceful. The lapping waves and the flowing lines of her robe give a sense of movement, which by contrast bring out the serenity and balance of the figure even more.

Although there are many different forms of Kuan Yin, this one has several typical features. Chinese culture being rather more decorous than Indian, Kuan Yin is always dressed in flowing garments, unlike some of the more scantily-clad Indian Bodhisattva princesses. The flowing lines of the folds of her robe often provide one of the most attractive aspects of images of her made of porcelain or other materials. Her head is often covered, and she generally has jewel ornaments, though in some figures the jewels disappear, giving her more of a nun's simplicity.

The waves playing around the base of the figure emphasize Kuan Yin's association with water. Until the middle of the twentieth century, statues of Kuan Yin were found all over China. These statues and shrines were very often placed near flowing water, overlooking a lake, or by the seashore. One also frequently finds images of Kuan Yin standing on a large lotus, travelling across the sea. These evoke the common Buddhist idea of being ferried across to the farther shore of nirvana by Kuan Yin. In general, too, we often talk of compassion as flowing, or as an outpouring from the heart, so it is not surprising that the end-lessly kind Kuan Yin should be associated with water.

The link of Kuan Yin with water is carried over into the idea that she has a specific divine abode. This is identified with P'u T'o Shan, an island in the South China Sea off the coast of Chekiang. Kuan Yin is often represented seated on a rock and looking out across the water.

Some of the forms of Kuan Yin are very closely based on those of Avalokiteshvara. For instance there are Kuan Yin 'Holder of the Lotus', and 'Lion's Roar' Kuan Yin, who is represented sit-ting on the back of a lion. These forms correspond to two well-known Indian forms of Avalokiteshvara.[41]

Some forms of Kuan Yin are flanked by two attendants: Lung Nu, the Dragon Maiden, who holds a giant pearl, and a smiling boy called Shan Ts'ai. He is the Chinese equivalent of Sudhana, the young hero of the *Gandavyuha Sutra*, one of the great Indian Buddhist texts, which tells how he visits over fifty teachers in order to learn how to follow the way of the Bodhisattva.

Kuan Yin is also frequently represented holding a child. This probably derives from a famous hymn of praise to Avalokit-eshvara in the *Lotus Sutra* – one of the most important texts for Chinese Buddhism. In this hymn it is said that Avalokiteshvara grants children to those of his devotees who desire them, so this form of Kuan Yin is known as the giver of children. These statues have sometimes been referred to as the Chinese Madonna and Chil. Indeed, some early Christian missionaries to China mis-took her for the Virgin Mary, and believed they had uncovered a native form of Chinese Christianity.

As is often the case, Kuan Yin was sometimes worshipped for reasons that had little to do with the path to Enlightenment, such as for curing infertility or granting success in purely worldly matters. As she was seen as the embodiment of kindness and compassion, she was very close to the everyday lives of her devotees, and was invoked in any kind of trouble, spiritual or material. She also became associated with various local goddesses and, in Japan, eventually found a place in Shintoism as well as Buddhism.

Avalokiteshvara is often depicted with many arms and heads. These symbolize his compassion reaching out to all situations, and his panoramic awareness of the needs of sentient beings. Kuan Yin is often represented similarly. She also often holds different emblems. (John Blofeld gives a list of forty-two of them.[42]) We have already seen her holding the slender vase of immortality. Longevity and immortality were great concerns of Indian and Chinese Taoist yogas, and in Tantric Buddhism they are particularly associated with the Lotus family. In Chapter 2 we saw that White Tara and Vijaya form an important triad of long-life deities with Amitayus, a form of Amitabha. So Kuan Yin has taken over the emblem of Amitayus, the nectar vase that bestows immortality.

Some forms of Kuan Yin can be a little reminiscent of Tara. For instance there is a form known as Willow Kuan Yin, who holds her left hand palm outwards in front of her heart like Tara. This form is usually shown seated under a willow tree, holding a willow stem in her right hand. As part of Kuan Yin's forty-two emblems, the willow branch is said to drive away sickness. Sometimes she holds the nectar-vase in one hand and the willow branch in the other. The nectar is said to be the 'sweet dew' of wisdom and compassion, and she is using the willow branch as a sprinkler in order to rain it down on the heads of those who call on her aid.

As I have already suggested, Kuan Yin's beauty has led to some of the finest productions of Chinese art. The depictions in porcelain of the White-Robed Kuan Yin in particular can achieve an extraordinary delicacy and refinement. In this way alone, she has had a considerable influence on Chinese culture. But her influence goes far deeper than in painting and sculpture; she was worshipped in temples all over China (as well as Korea and Japan) for more than a thousand years, especially during the three festivals devoted to her in the course of the year. For all those hundreds of years she was meditated upon, and chants in her honour were recited. All the main forms of devotion to Avalokiteshvara can also apply to Kuan Yin. The P'u Men chapter of the *Lotus Sutra*, which deals with Avalokiteshvara, may be recited, as well as chants such as *namo kuan shih yin pu-sa*: 'Homage to the Bodhisattva Kuan Yin'.[43]

The fact that many of the forms of devotion that were used for the male Avalokiteshvara were applied equally to the female forms of Kuan Yin shows that on advanced spiritual levels gender is not a major issue at all. On the ordinary human level of development our minds are strongly influenced by being associated with a male or a female body – both directly, through different hormones affecting us, and indirectly, through being conditioned by different cultural assumptions about men and women. But the path to Enlightenment involves freeing ourselves from being conditioned in this way. When someone sees the true nature of things, the *dharmakaya*, they find that they have transcended gender distinctions. This is expressed in the following verse:

> *The Dharma-body of Kuan-yin*
> *Is neither male nor female.*
> *Even the body is not a body,*
> *What attributes can there be? …*
> *Let it be known unto all Buddhists:*
> *Do not cling to form.*
> *The Bodhisattva is you:*
> *Not the picture or the image.*[44]

# CONCLUSION

The figures we have met in this book express the qualities of Enlightenment through a tremendous range of appearances and archetypes. The mature and beautiful Prajnaparamita, whose body is a galaxy of golden Buddhas, seems to be transcendental wisdom expressing itself through the form of the Great Mother. In the forms of old crones or witches, Shridevi and Ekajata protect the Dharma, and the mind of the Buddhist practitioner. The beautiful Tara is said to embody all the positive qualities of a virgin, a queen, and a mother. The consorts of the Five Buddhas are very much 'Queens of the Mandala'.

Western women may well find the dakinis particularly exciting expressions of Enlightenment. It is a cliché that Christianity has tended to present women with two alternatives: the Madonna or the whore, the Virgin Mary or Mary Magdalen. This has often caused the more passionate side of women to be cast into the 'outer darkness'. But in Buddhist Tantra the wild, naked, dishevelled dakinis are as much expressions of Enlightened consciousness as the calm and serene White Tara. The dakinis have something magical about them, as well as the scent of danger. Thus they touch upon not only something of the Wild Woman but also the Shamaness or Magician, as well as the fearless Warrior and the passionate Lover.

This tremendous spectrum of different figures is united by two factors. First, they all help to lead those who reflect and meditate on them towards Enlightenment. The Buddha once said that his teaching was like the great ocean; from whichever part of the ocean you take water, it always tastes of salt. Similarly, he said, whichever aspect of the Dharma you learn has the taste of freedom. These female deities are all embodiments of the Dharma and, peaceful or wrathful, beautiful or ugly, they can all lead us in the direction of liberation from suffering.

The second factor that unites the figures is that they are all insubstantial – emanations of emptiness. When you meditate on any of them, you do not begin by seeing the figure herself; you start by visualizing a vast expanse of sky, stretching away in all directions. The figure then appears in the sky. She is made of light, like a hologram or something fashioned out of rainbows. At the end of the meditation, you imagine her dissolving back into the blue sky. All these meditations are, so to speak, dramatized enactments of the nature of reality. The blue sky symbolizes the open dimension of being – that nothing has any fixed core but is a dynamic process, appearing, changing, and disappearing as conditions change. Even though you may have visualized a wonderful figure of great beauty, even though you may have felt you were in the presence of deep love and wisdom, the figure dissolves away at the end of the meditation.

Not only is the deity insubstantial, but you, the meditator, are also of the nature of emptiness, a dynamic process with no fixed core. This is why although in some forms of meditation you see the figure appear in the sky in front of you, in others you actually imagine yourself as her. You see your physical body replaced by one of coloured light, adorned perhaps with silks and jewels. (And in Tantric Buddhism these practices are done by both men and women – so a man may visualize himself in a woman's form, or vice versa. As well as the more profound benefits, this also helps to loosen attachment to gender identity.)

The fact that all the figures are insubstantial, born from the sky, should help prevent us from fixing them, pigeonholing them into some neat mental category. The fact that they can be visualized internally or externally should help us see that finally they are neither 'in here' nor 'out there'. Visualizing these figures actually helps to break down our rigid tendency to experience everything in terms of a dichotomy between subject and object. When you visualize a subtle radiant form in front of you, you are working on the subject–object divide by refining the object. When you see yourself as a figure made of light, you are refining the subject, what you think of as 'you'.

I hope that in this short book I have been able to convey something of the beauty and richness of these female deities, and that you will feel inspired to explore further, for there is plenty more literature available. But just reading about these figures is like reading a description of wonderful stained glass windows, which can only give us some idea of how they look. We really need to encounter these beautiful and inspiring figures for ourselves, to go and look at the reds and the blues, the flowing illuminated outlines of the figures themselves. Buddhists through the ages have done this by practising meditation, encountering these figures within their own minds, and allowing the power, freedom, and love of the deity to speak to them directly.

Finally, though, we need to recognize that, like stained glass, these figures are nothing in themselves, they are vehicles for the magic of light and colour. The source of that magic lies far beyond them, in the vast blue sky. Through deep meditation it is possible to go beyond reliance even on these Buddhist forms, to travel into the blue sky, and recognize the radiant, shining nature of mind itself.

# NOTES AND REFERENCES

1   Trevor Leggett (trans.), *A First Zen Reader*, Charles E. Tuttle,
    Rutland vt 1960, p.67.

2   His full name is Avalokiteshvara: 'the lord who looks down'. This
    is understood to mean that he is looking over the world with a
    compassionate gaze. In Tibetan he is called Chenrezig.

3   Sanskrit: Dundubhīśvara

4   This story is told in *The Golden Rosary: a History Illuminating the
    Origin of the Tantra of Tārā* by Tāranātha, a scholar of the now
    defunct Jonang school of Tibetan Buddhism, translated by Martin
    Willson in *In Praise of Tārā*, Wisdom Publications, London 1986,
    pp.33–6 and pp.178–206.

5   Stephan Beyer, *The Cult of Tārā: Magic and Ritual in Tibet*,
    University of California Press, Berkeley 1978, p.449. These three
    *vimokshas*, or 'releases', are 'the signless', 'the desireless', and
    'emptiness of inherent existence'. They are transcendental states
    arrived at by meditating on, respectively, the impermanence, the
    unsatisfactoriness, and the insubstantiality of mundane life.

6   The tradition of White Tara as a conferrer of longevity goes back to
    ancient India when an Indian teacher called Vagishvarakirti
    ('famed lord of speech') wrote a set of three texts around White
    Tara called 'Cheating Death'.

7   Buddhism believes in rebirth. According to the tradition there are various realms into which one can be reborn, of which the human realm is considered the best basis from which to gain Enlightenment.

8   These conditions are discussed in *The Cult of Tārā*, op. cit., pp.367–8.

9   *Dhammapada* 114

10  One of the epithets of Enlightenment is that it is *amṛta* (in Sanskrit, *amata* in Pali), which means deathless.

11  The Wheel of Life (Sanskrit: *bhavacakra*) is a traditional Buddhist teaching picture, showing how we set ourselves up to suffer in life after life through craving, aversion, and ignorance. By extension, it is the whole process of unenlightened existence itself. See Kulananda, *The Wheel of Life*, Windhorse Publications, Birmingham 2000.

12  See Chapter 9 of Vessantara, *Meeting the Buddhas: a Guide to Buddhas, Bodhisattvas, and Tantric Deities*, Windhorse Publications, Birmingham 1998; or Chapter 5 of Vessantara, *The Mandala of the Five Buddhas*, Windhorse Publications, Birmingham 1999.

13  See Chapter 8 of *Meeting the Buddhas*, op. cit.; or Chapter 4 of *The Mandala of the Five Buddhas*, op. cit.

14  According to one tradition, the lineage of her teaching began with the Indian siddha Nagarjuna, and was subsequently passed on to the great Tantric master Padmasambhava, who was crucial to the establishment of Buddhism in Tibet in the eighth century. His female disciple Yeshe Tsogyal subsequently hid, for the benefit of future generations, teachings about the meditation of Red Tara. Hidden teachings of this kind are being found up to the present day, and a cycle of Red Tara teachings was found in the last century by Apong Terton. These meditations continue to be practised in both the Nyingma and Sakya schools of Tibetan Buddhism.

15  Red Tara's three eyes are traditionally said to represent the three *kāyas* of a Buddha. These are the three levels on which one can

experience a Buddha: their physical body, their archetypal form, and the absolute reality they have realized. For an explanation of these three kayas, see *Meeting the Buddhas*, op. cit., pp.27–30.

16 The first tradition is associated with Nagarjuna, and often with Atisha; the second is a Nyingma tradition attributed to Longchenpa (1308–63); the third one, which is less frequently encountered, is associated with the seventh-century Indian master Suryagupta.

17 The first two verses of the 'Homage to the Twenty-One Tārās', translated by Stephan Beyer in *The Cult of Tārā*, op. cit., pp.211–12.

18 These are known in Sanskrit as the *aṣṭamaṅgala*. They are the parasol, the golden fishes, the treasure vase, the lotus, the right-turning conch shell, the endless knot, the victory banner, and the wheel. See Dagyab Rinpoche, *Buddhist Symbols in Tibetan Culture*, Wisdom Publications, Somerville 1995.

19 Vijaya's full name is Ushnisha Vijaya. The *ushnisha* is the protrusion on the top of the head that is found on many images of the Buddha.

20 Originally a burial mound erected over the remains of the Buddha and other great teachers, the stupa gained increasing symbolic associations over time, linking it to many aspects of Buddhist teaching.

21 This figure is known in Sanskrit as Prajñāpāramitā. The Tibetan rendering is Sherapkyi Pharoltuchinma.

22 This is the opening line of the *Ratnaguṇasaṁcayagāthā*, the verse summary of the *Perfection of Wisdom in 8,000 Lines*.

23 Literally 'garland'; the Tibetan is *trhengwa*.

24 Edward Conze (trans.), *Buddhist Wisdom Books, containing the Diamond Sutra and the Heart Sutra*, Unwin Hyman, London 1988, pp.123–9.

25 Ibid., p.21.

26 From Rāhulabhadra's 'Hymn to Perfect Wisdom', ed. trans. Edward Conze, *Buddhist Texts through the Ages*, Oneworld, Oxford

1995, p.147 (slightly adapted). 'Tathāgata' is another title of the Buddha.

27 In some later Tantric texts, Akshobhya and Vairocana swap positions, so that Vairocana is in the east, and Akshobhya in the centre. Akshobhya's consort when he is the central figure is called Vajradhatvisvari: 'sovereign lady of the diamond sphere'.

28 Or, in some versions of the practice, a vase of treasure.

29 The eightfold path consists of right vision, right emotion, right speech, right action, right livelihood, right effort, right mindfulness, and right concentration.

30 This is a reference to the four great elements of earth, water, fire, and air, known in Sanskrit as *mahābhūtas*, which can also mean 'great ghosts'.

31 Generosity, ethics, patience, effort, meditation, and wisdom.

32 Vajravarahi is of particular importance for the Kagyu school of Tibetan Buddhism.

33 Heruka is also often referred to Cakrasamvara. He is a semi-wrathful form of Avalokita, the Bodhisattva of compassion.

34 Anon.

35 Yeshe Tsogyal, *The Life and Liberation of Padmasambhava*, Dharma Publishing, Berkeley 1978, p.635.

36 Meditation on Shridevi was introduced into Tibet by Sangwa Sherap, and to begin with she played an important part in the practice of the Sakya school.

37 Robert Thurman, *Essential Tibetan Buddhism*, HarperCollins, San Francisco 1996, p.276.

38 Tibetan: Tsechikma or Ralchikma.

39 René de Nebesky-Wojkowitz, *Oracles and Demons of Tibet*, SMC Publishing, Taipei, n.d., pp.33–4.

40 Translated by the Dzogchen Community, adapted by the author.

41 These two forms are known as Padmapani and Simhanada respectively. (The Sanskrit has the same meaning as the Chinese in both cases.)

42 See John Blofeld, *In Search of the Goddess of Compassion: the Mystical Cult of Kuan Yin*, Unwin Paperbacks, London 1990, p.151.

43 More literally, this chant means 'Homage to the Bodhisattva who hears the cries of the world'. John Blofeld gives a slightly longer version: *Namu ta-tzu ta-pei Kuan Shih Yin P'u-Sa* ('Homage to the greatly compassionate, greatly merciful Kuan Shih Yin Bodhisattva!').

44 Quoted in C. N. Tay, 'Kuan-yin: the Cult of Half Asia', *History of Religions* 16 (1976–7), p.173.

# SELECTED READING

## General
Vessantara, *Meeting the Buddhas: a Guide to Buddhas, Bodhisattvas, and Tantric Deities*, Windhorse Publications, Birmingham 1998

## Tara
Stephan Beyer, *The Cult of Tārā: Magic and Ritual in Tibet*, University of California Press, Berkeley 1978
Bokar Rinpoche, *Tara The Feminine Divine*, ClearPoint Press, San Francisco 1999.
Jane Tromge, *Red Tara Commentary: compiled from the Teachings of Chagdud Tulku*, Padma Publishing, Junction City 1994
Martin Willson, *In Praise of Tārā: Songs to the Saviouress*, Wisdom Publications, London 1986

## Perfect Wisdom
Edward Conze (trans.), *Buddhist Wisdom Books, containing the Diamond Sutra and the Heart Sutra*, Unwin Hyman, London 1988
Edward Conze, 'The Iconography of the Prajñāpāramitā', in *Thirty Years of Buddhist Studies*, Bruno Cassirer, Oxford 1967, pp.242–60

## Five Prajnas
Padmasambhava, *The Tibetan Book of the Dead*, trans. Robert Thurman, Aquarian Press, London 1994

## The Dakini

Elizabeth English, *Vajrayoginī: Her Visualization, Rituals and Forms*, Wisdom Books, Boston 2002

Nam-mkha'i snying-po, *Mother of Knowledge: The Enlightenment of Ye-shes mTsho-rgyal*, Dharma Publishing, Berkeley 1983

Judith Simmer-Brown, *Dakini's Warm Breath: The Feminine Principle in Tibetan Buddhism*, Shambhala, Boston 2001

## Female Protectors

René de Nebesky-Wojkowitz, *Oracles and Demons of Tibet: the Cult and Iconography of the Tibetan Protective Deities*, SMC Publishing, Taipei n.d.

## Kuan Yin

John Blofeld, *In Search of the Goddess of Compassion: the Mystical Cult of Kuan Yin*, Unwin Paperbacks, London 1990

Sandy Boucher, *Discovering Kwan Yin, Buddhist Goddess of Compassion*, Beacon Press, Boston 1999

Martin Palmer and Jay Ramsay with Man-Ho Kwok, *Kuan Yin: Myths and Revelations of the Chinese Goddess of Compassion*, Thorsons, London and San Francisco 1995

# INDEX

**WINDHORSE PUBLICATIONS**

Windhorse Publications is a Buddhist charitable company based in the UK. We place
great emphasis on producing books of high quality that are accessible and relevant to
those interested in Buddhism at whatever level. We are the main publisher of the works
of Sangharakshita, the founder of the Triratna Buddhist Order and Community. Our
books draw on the whole range of the Buddhist tradition, including translations of
traditional texts, commentaries, books that make links with contemporary culture and
ways of life, biographies of Buddhists, and works on meditation.

As a not-for-profit enterprise, we ensure that all surplus income is invested in new
books and improved production methods, to better communicate Buddhism in the 21st
century. We welcome donations to help us continue our work – to find out more, go to
windhorsepublications.com.

The Windhorse is a mythical animal that flies over the earth carrying on its back three
precious jewels, bringing these invaluable gifts to all humanity: the Buddha (the
'awakened one'), his teaching, and the community of all his followers.

Windhorse Publications
38 Newmarket Road
Cambridge CB5 8DT
info@windhorsepublications.com

Consortium Book Sales & Distribution
210 American Drive
Jackson TN 38301
USA

Windhorse Books
PO Box 574
Newtown NSW 2042
Australia

## THE TRIRATNA BUDDHIST COMMUNITY

Windhorse Publications is a part of the Triratna Buddhist Community, an international movement with centres in Europe, India, North and South America and Australasia. At these centres, members of the Triratna Buddhist Order offer classes in meditation and Buddhism. Activities of the Triratna Community also include retreat centres, residential spiritual communities, ethical Right Livelihood businesses, and the Karuna Trust, a UK fundraising charity that supports social welfare projects in the slums and villages of India.

Through these and other activities, Triratna is developing a unique approach to Buddhism, not simply as a philosophy and a set of techniques, but as a creatively directed way of life for all people living in the conditions of the modern world.

If you would like more information about Triratna please visit thebuddhistcentre.com or write to:

London Buddhist Centre
51 Roman Road
London E2 0HU
UK
contact@lbc.org.uk

Aryaloka
14 Heartwood Circle
Newmarket NH 03857
USA
info@aryaloka.org

Sydney Buddhist Centre
24 Enmore Road
Sydney NSW 2042
Australia
info@sydneybuddhistcentre.org.au

**Sangharakshita: The Boy, the Monk, the Man**
*Nagabodhi*

A monk, a man, a writer, and a poet; founder of the Triratna Buddhist Order and Community – a pioneering worldwide Buddhist movement. An audacious reformer, and for some a deeply controversial figure. In an absorbing narrative, Nagabodhi takes us on a journey through the twists and turns of Sangharakshita's life; the experiences, insights, and reflections that nurtured his approach as a teacher; and the legacy he left behind.

'…*a wonderfully engaging account of the life and work of a remarkable man….*' — **Maitreyabandhu**, author of *Life with Full Attention* and founder of PoetryEast

'*He led the way in the West in creating a viable model of how a non-monastic sangha community could work – as well as among the Dalits in India. …a tremendous achievement requiring great vision, self-sacrifice, and determination, not to mention hard work, courage, patience, and perhaps one might say a certain degree of audacity….*' — **Lama Shenpen Hookham**, founder of the Awakened Heart Sangha and author of *The Buddha Within* and other titles

'Consistently subtle, perceptive, and engaging, this book is a vivid description of what it was like to be around Sangharakshita and a perceptive account of Sangharakshita's growing understanding of what it means to live an authentic Buddhist life….' — **Vishvapani Blomfield**, author of *Gautama Buddha: The Life and Teachings of the Awakened One*

Nagabodhi joined Sangharakshita's new Buddhist Order in 1974 and has given his life to a range of Triratna projects in the UK and abroad. He worked closely with Sangharakshita, sometimes living in communities with him. In 1982 they travelled on tour in India, an adventure Nagabodhi chronicled in *Jai Bhim! Dispatches from a Peaceful Revolution*.

ISBN 978-1-911407-97-3
384 pages

**Meeting the Buddhas: A Guide to Buddhas, Bodhisattvas, and Tantric Deities**
*Vessantara*

'*The Mahāyāna pantheon is replete with archetypal divinities and goddesses, myth-models, avatars and super-heroes, saints and sages of all genders…. You too can delve into and delight in this marvellous, uplifting vision of the luminous reality….*' — **Lama Surya Das**

'*The depth of Vessantara's own practice and comfort in visionary realms means this book is an invitation to experience our lives infused with imagination, light, love, power, and mystery.*' — **Vidyamala Burch**, OBE

'*This wonderful book was an absolute treasure trove for me…. A gift of wisdom and inspiration.*' — **Professor Paul Gilbert**, OBE, author of *The Compassionate Mind*

'*I find myself in another world, as I read this book…. Here is a path for Buddhist practice, which engages the heart as well as the mind.*' — **Dr Elizabeth English** (Locana)

'*…a wonderfully rich, comprehensive, and thorough exploration of the world of Buddhist Vajrayāna….*' — **Rob Preece**, author of *The Psychology of Buddhist Tantra*

*Meeting the Buddhas* is a modern classic, giving a vivid and accessible introduction to all the main meditation figures in the Indo-Tibetan Buddhist tradition. It is a mine of information for those who want to learn about buddhas, bodhisattvas, and tantric deities, and of inspiration for those who are already engaged in the practices.

Vessantara powerfully evokes the figures, giving the reader a real feeling for what it's like to meditate on them, and how they can transform us on a deep level. It gives detailed descriptions of the figures, including their mudras and symbolic emblems, so it can be used as a handy reference to identify and learn about particular images.

First published in 1993, this revised one-volume edition has over 50 illustrations, including 27 colour plates, to help you recognize and connect with the figures.

Rich, clear, and inspiring, this book is the perfect companion for anyone who wants to know about, or practise deeply with, these powerful and transformative figures.

ISBN 978-1-911407-87-4
456 pages

**I Hear Her Words: An Introduction to Women in Buddhism**
*Alice Collett*

Is there gender equality in Buddhist traditions? What do Buddhist texts say about women? This book offers a new introduction to women in Buddhism, and gives unique access to the more rarely told histories of the many inspiring Buddhist women who fought against constraint. In this book we hear about and from many Buddhist women, disciples and teachers, their wisdom and their practice.

*'This is a thorough, comprehensive and well researched guide to the history and agency of women in Buddhism. We travel widely through time and space, discovering awakened and well-practised women of old to the present day.'* — **Martine Batchelor** is the author of *Women on the Buddhist Path* and *Women in Korean Zen*

*'This wide-ranging and innovative introduction to women in Buddhism draws on sources from across the Buddhist world to interrogate the idea that Buddhism views women as inferior to men. The author's blending of scholarly analysis and stories of women's lives makes this book a valuable addition to the growing body of work about women in Buddhism.'* — **Danasamudra**, co-founder of the Triratna Women Project and Librarian of the Sangharakshita Library

*'Written in a clear and accessible style, this book offers an excellent introduction into how women have shaped Buddhism from its beginning in India and over the course of its historical development throughout the Buddhist world.'* — **Martin Seeger**, Professor of Thai Studies at the University of Leeds, author of *Gender and the Path to Awakening*

*'A sweeping survey of Buddhist women in Asia from historical times to the present, showing their personal and societal struggles, their many contributions, and their unique wisdom.'* — **Judith Simmer-Brown**, Distinguished Professor of Naropa University and author of *Dakini's Warm Breath: The Feminine Principle in Tibetan Buddhism*

Alice Collett is an academic who specializes in women in Indian Buddhism. Her books include *Women in Early Indian Buddhism: Comparative Textual Studies* (2013) and *Lives of Early Buddhist Nuns: Biographies as History* (2016).

ISBN 978-1-911407-71-3
280 pages

**Change Your Mind**

*Paramananda*

An accessible and thorough guide, this best-seller introduces two Buddhist meditations and deals imaginatively with practical difficulties, meeting distraction and doubt with determination and humour.

*Inspiring, calming and friendly ... If you've always thought meditation might be a good idea, but found other step-by-step guides lacking in spirit, this book could finally get you going.* — *Here's Health*

ISBN 9781-899579-75-4
208 pages

**Uncontrived Mindfulness: Ending Suffering through Attention, Curiosity and Wisdom**
*Vajradevi*

*Uncontrived Mindfulness* is a fresh and comprehensive guide to awareness of how the mind shapes experience. The Buddha emphasized that happiness is found through understanding the mind rather than getting caught up in sense experience. This simple yet radical shift is key to a relaxed and uncontrived way of practising. Freedom comes from uniting right view and mindfulness.

A deep dive into the practice of exploring our experience as it happens, Vajradevi's emphasis is on cultivating wisdom, using the tools of attention, curiosity and discernment to recognize and see through the delusion that is causing our suffering.

Vajradevi is a warm and insightful guide to this exploration, drawing on her intensive and wide-ranging practice of satipaṭṭhāna meditation. The clear explanations and instructions are amplified by Vajradevi's personal accounts, charting her uncompromising voyage into self-discovery. Guided meditations are included.

*'Vajradevi is a practitioner who shares her own experience of practising mindfulness simply and clearly. She makes traditional concepts accessible because she knows them from the inside, and this book is full of stories of how Vajradevi has learned to be mindful of her own life.'* — **Vishvapani Blomfield**, author of *Gautama Buddha: The Life and Teachings of the Awakened One*

*'A wonderful book, written with that independence of mind characteristic of deep practitioners.'* — **Kamalashila**, meditation teacher and author of *Buddhist Meditation: Tranquillity, Imagination & Insight*

*'Vajradevi gives relevant and real examples which show us that dedicating ourselves to mindfulness does not mean being cut off from life. I loved reading the stories she weaves in to explain her journey in mindfulness and the thoughtful connections she makes with common doubts or questions about the practice, the journey, and its effects.'* — **Ma Thet,** translator for Sayadaw U Tejaniya

Vajradevi grew up on the Isle of Wight and met the Dharma at the age of 23. She was ordained into the Triratna Buddhist Order in 1995. For the past twenty years she has explored and taught meditation based on the *Satipaṭṭhāna Sutta*, the Buddha's primary teaching on mindfulness. She spent a year in Myanmar on retreat with Sayadaw U Tejaniya, and leads retreats in the UK and Europe that teach mindfulness as a path to wisdom.

ISBN 978-1-911407-61-4
248 pages